BOSSIN' UP

*Snatching Back My Power
Through God's Process*

Ke'Arra Kelly

Copyright © 2019 by Ke'Arra Nunnery.

All rights reserved, including the right to reproduce this book or portions thereof in any form whatsoever. For more information address The Literary Revolutionary, YBF Publishing LLC.
PO Box 361526 Decatur, GA 30036

ISBN #: 978-1-950279-12-8

Edited by: Anje McLish
Editor-in-Chief: Nia Sade Akinyemi, The Literary Revolutionary
Cover Design by: Farrah Gregg-Carlos

Manufactured in the United States of America

For information regarding special discounts for bulk purchases, please contact The Literary Revolutionary Special Sales Team at 470-396-0660 or support@theliteraryrevolutionary.com

Follow Ke'Arra!

**Instagram: @sweetkearra
@bossinher20s**

Table of Contents

Acknowledgments — 9

Introduction: Bossin' Letter — 13

Chapter 1: Power — 24

Chapter 2: The Process — 40

Chapter 3: 20s — 58

Chapter 4: God's Plans vs. My Plans — 84

Chapter 5: Silent Season — 97

Chapter 6: Frenemies — 123

Chapter 7: Healing 101 — 141

Ending Letter: Walk in Your Truth — 161

About the Author   167

Dedicated To:

This book is dedicated to God. Thank you for this vision. I would not have been able to write this without the process you put me through to even have this wisdom. At times I did not understand, but I trusted you.
I also dedicate this book to my Granny, thank you for all the times you took me to church, and answered all my crazy questions about the Word. Continue to cover me.

Acknowledgements

This book wouldn't have happened of course without God putting a seed in me that eventually grew into me having the wisdom to share with Bossin' women around the world. I am thankful for you to be even reading my book. I am thankful for the amazing people who have been on this journey with me. To the people that have helped me in many ways than they even know. Thank you for seeing something in me at times when I couldn't see it in myself. Thank you to my mom. Thank you for being the strong example and giving birth to the cutest, sassiest, most intelligent Bossin' thing to walk this earth (me) and helping me navigate through life. Thank you for always supporting everything I do, even my craziest ideas. Thank you to my sister and brother who always cheer me on as well. Thank you for being there for me making me smile when I felt I had no one else. You both will forever be my best-friends. Thank you to my family. Thank you all for your support and always cheering me on.

I am proud to say that I have a family who shows up and supports everything I do. There is nothing like family and I am thankful for mine: Harvey's, Kelly's, Nunnery's, Wilson's, Lunsford's, Burnside/Jones, Lopez's, and more. You guys always show up and show out for me. Y'all are the best. I would like to thank my boyfriend Marquis, thank you for pushing me so hard to finish what I started. Even when I would cry my eyes out about all my what ifs you stood by me and made sure I knew who the heck I was, and constantly reminded me that I had the power to finish this book. I will forever be thankful for that. I would like to thank one of best girlfriends Charisma for knowing about this book when it was just a small idea and encouraging me to go through with it. Thank you for your friendship throughout this journey Your friendship is very much appreciated. Thank you to my go-to Bennett sisters, Kee'Aera Hood, Mykia Bennett, Alexis Small, and Chanelle Gainey who have always been in my corner cheering me on and pushing me to my fullest potential. So thankful that our paths crossed. Most importantly, thank you to Nia Sade Akinyemi. Thank you for taking a chance on me. Thank you for teaching me the ins and outs of running a business properly. Showing me how important it is for a woman and especially a Black woman, to tell our stories. I will be forever thankful for you and helping me on this journey to making my book idea into a reality. You are heaven sent and I know God will keep using you to help other women of color share their stories as well.

Thank you to all who have supported me in everything that I do. You all are appreciated!

Much love,
Ke'Arra

BOSSIN' UP

Diggin' deep inside of who you are to take the necessary steps to do the inside work in order for God to elevate you to the next level.

Bossin' Letter

"Some things God takes you through are not for you, but it's so you can reach somebody else."
-- T.D. Jakes

Hey girl,

Is it okay if I call you girl? I'm writing this personal letter to you because today is the day you will take on a new journey. Today you're about to start Bossin' Up and Snatching Back Your Power. It is time! Let me start off by saying, if you were looking to feel connected to someone who totally gets all that you are going through right now in your twenties. I am her. She is me. I get it. You have been letting the past and current situations hold you back long enough. Life has done a whole 360 for you in these last couple of years, am I right? I know all about how that goes. The season you are in right now, may not be looking up. You may feel like God has forgotten all about you. It hurts. It may seem as *though everyone else's grass is greener on the other side while God still has you planting seeds on your raggedy side. Trust me, I know how that feels too. But see, when you're special God has to take His time with you. Those seeds need to be watered a little bit more for you to step into all of what God has for you. Maybe, you're just like me, and had to one day face yourself in the mirror and begin realizing that the only person that is holding you back from really going after what God has for you and wants for you to fully step into your Power, is really you. Facing that reality can be tough. But this season is your Bossin' Up season. Real Bossin' moves is when you recognize where you made the wrong turn, where you recognize you're letting your situations have a control over you and it is hindering you from what God is calling you to do. Real Bossin' moves is realizing it is time to get back you again and begin pressing in more to snatching back your power, but only with God's process. Now, that's real Bossin'. This season of your life God is trying to elevate you to the next level in your life, but He cannot do that with you standing in your own way.*

**The question is:
Are you ready to begin Bossin Up' and get up out of your own way?**

On my own journey I've had amazing moments, but I've also had the not so pretty moments. The real Bossin' Up moments that no one speaks of. It's those moments you try not to talk about and avoid like plague. They aren't picture perfect worthy to post on social media. It's those moments where you had to dig deep into yourself and face those issues that you secretly deal with. I am talking the real tears, feeling like the world is collapsing, and no one is in your corner but God, Bossin' Up. I get it. You are me; I am you. I've been there. In a world full of social media posts telling you if you aren't doing this or that you aren't making "boss moves." I've come to terms that Boss moves doesn't necessarily always mean being successful and being on the scene. Boss moves can also mean diggin' deep inside of who you are and realizing the areas where you need to begin doing the inside work. I am here not to only share my personal journey of Bossin' Up my life, but also to help you identify areas in your life that you may need to begin Bossin Up in as well. This book Bossin' Up is all about doing the inside work.

'Bossin' Up: Snatching Back Your Power' breaks down the power of God not only in my life, but the power that He has in your life as well.

Through your own journey of Bossin' Up and learning how to snatch back your own power through the process that God has you on you will see first-hand as well as learn some tips on how I snatched back my power through God's process.

- *Learning to heal from past experiences*
- *Beginning to let go of certain relationships*
- *Journey of self-discovery and at times re-self-discovery*
- *Building a stronger connection to God*
- *Following God's plan vs. your own plans*
- *Building unshakable faith*
- *all while learning how to snatch back ALL YOUR POWER from situations that happened in your life that one day made me wake up and not feel like myself.*

That is definitely what I call making Bossin' moves!

I know through this journey of not only God's process but being in your twenties it can feel like a lonely rollercoaster ride. It may seem like no one understands you or the things you might face. A lot of times our issues we face may get swept under the rug because, "Oh you're young you have no idea" but trust me what you are facing in your twenties MATTER. The depression you may be going through, matters. The loneliness and isolation you feel, matters. Your healing, matters. Your voice, matters. You are not on an island all alone facing these issues on your own. Yes, at times it may feel that way. However, this book will show you I too understand all of what you may be facing. I may not be going through the same exact thing as you, but what I can do is show you that I too am going through those moments that we do not so willingly share. I can show you how I began Bossin' Up through my own tough experiences. This is a sisterhood, girl you are not alone. In Bossin' Up I will share experiences of my life that I haven't shared with anyone, but you. I will break down the real about my process of Bossin' Up and Snatching back my power through God's Process and how many times I wanted the towel in. GIRL! I will give you the real about my healing process, the tears I've cried, and my personal connection to God through it all. You will feel so connected to me, that you will no longer feel alone, but know for sure that there is someone (hint: me, girl) out there that had gone through the same thing, and at times still going through it. I am not making anything cute and pretty in here. I am giving you the real. I am sharing my truth. And hopefully helping you to one day share your own and lift up someone else to do the same. Through sharing my journey my goal is to help you to recognize the area in your life where you too need to start Bossin' Up and Snatching back your power! I know you feel alone when you have to deal with past experiences, ending toxic friendships, holding onto guilt, trying to navigate life after college, or even just trying to get back to YOU again. I know, and I understand. I've been there. I know all about the tears you cried, the betrayal you felt, the times you didn't feel like you anymore. I get it. I've been there, too. Hell, sometimes I still am there. Sometimes I still battle with those feelings. You find yourself having to put back the pieces that you gave away so easily. The process can be one lonely and hard (emphasis on LONELY and HARD) journey, but it is necessary! And I want you to know that I am right there with you. So many of us are facing similar issues that we do not speak about. I am just like you too; I am still trying to figure this thing called life out as a twenty-four-year-old. I too am learning how to snatch back my power from things and people that I've given it away to so freely. And if I am being honest, between us girls, I am learning and at times I am failing

(another way of learning because you truly never fail) but I am figuring it out, and I want to help you

begin your process. But this time, you aren't alone. I'm on this journey with you. It is time to start recognizing when you began to start letting your power go. It is time to start identifying where you need to begin your healing and start Bossin' Up and Snatching Back Your Power, girl!

This book is your safe place. This book is your built-in girlfriend, who has a shoulder for you to cry on and give you all the tea about navigating these twenties at the same damn time. This process God takes you on in order for you to begin Bossin' Up is never easy, and can at times, well majority of the time be uncomfortable, but it is necessary in order for God to elevate you in to the next level He is trying to get you to.

* *

I am proud of you for taking the first steps to recognize that there are areas that you may need to begin Bossin' Up in. I am proud of you for sticking through the Process that God is putting you through to get to the other side and trust me you will get to the other side. You are not alone this time, you have a friend (hint: me, girl) who understands, who has been there, at time still there, and who knows the real behind it all. So, we will take on this process *together, and I will share my personal stories with you and help you get started with BOSSIN UP your own life... because I mean, that's what girlfriends do right? (You are basically my bestie now, so just accept it!)*

Let me be honest with you though, you may have to get vulnerable and share and heal parts of you that you tried so desperately to tuck away, just like I did. (no judgment here)

So, these are the things I'm going to need from you:

1. **You to be willing to be real with yourself:**
   Honesty is key with this book. You will need to be very transparent. Get real about what and who has hurt you. What are you still hurting from? What are the things you need to snatch back your power from? Is God trying to plant you in this season and you are running from the process? What is it that you feel?

2. ***Opening Up***
   The only way if this friendship is going to work girl, is if you open up. I know, I know it's not the easiest. Especially if you

struggle with trusting others. But in order to heal and begin your process of Bossin' Up and snatching back the power that belongs to you, you will need to have the willingness to open up and tell your truth.

3. Being Vulnerable

Now being open and vulnerable can go hand in hand and I know they both are equally hard. You may view being vulnerable as a weakness; but it is the exact opposite. (Don't worry I felt the same way before; would even say things like "girl, I don't cry that's whack" HA!) Vulnerability is where your healing will begin. Cry it out. Let it be known you are still hurt and don't have it all together. Being vulnerable just means you are stronger than you think! Trust me, being vulnerable during this process helps a bunch!

4. Challenge yourself to do these exercises to begin your Bossin' Up: Snatching Back your Power process

There will be exercises that will help you get through this process. It may be tough to go back and write some of these things out but remember the end goal. You are doing this to heal yourself. These challenges will help you identify what in your life needs a little bit of Bossin' Up!

You are enough and are worthy of Bossin' Up your life. You are worthy of being healed from past experiences. You are worthy to snatch back all your power. I need you to know this time around you are NOT alone. No, the healing process is never easy. Just when you find yourself getting over one healing process here comes another. But, don't worry you can get through. There may be times where you may not want to complete an exercise because revisiting a situation brings you pain, it is okay. Just remember that I am here alongside you. I am here to help guide you through this process and make you feel as though you have a safe space to express what you are going through with no judgment. I can guarantee, after hearing some of my breakthroughs from my own journey of self-discovery and healing you will want to dig deep into your own journey of Bossin' Up.

It is time you reclaim authority over your life and look those very things that took your power straight in the eye and remind them, "Nah girl, this is MY peace and I am snatching it back! This is MY confidence and I am snatching it back! This is MY happiness and I am snatching it back. It all belongs to me!"

Take your time and constantly remind yourself:

I AM WORTHY TO BEGIN BOSSIN UP MY LIFE AND SNATCHING BACK ALL MY POWER!

Now let's get started with you Bossin' Up your life!

Love your new bestie, Ke'Arra Kelly

CHAPTER 1: POWER

"Your personal power is not something that is going to reveal itself at some later date. Your power is a result of your decision to reveal it. You are powerful in whatever moment you choose to be."

-- Marianne Williamson

WHAT IS POWER?

Power can be identified as a lot of things for many different people. Some may identify power as who is higher up in a position and has the say so in the building. Power can be described as someone who has influence. Power can be going as far as discussing identity and dealing with certain races and sexes having power over another individual. Power can even come to play when discussing money. There are so many ways to identify this one word. One thing we can agree on is that when you think of power, you think of authority. In this book when I speak of power, I am speaking of the power that was given to you by God. This is with or without you knowing you have authority over your life. You have that power to speak and walk in your authority.

You have that kind of power that is always within you. That power that makes you, you. That kind of power is something we all possess deep down. It comes easy to you. See your power can be:

- Your willingness to forgive others
- Your happiness
- Your positive mindset

- Your confidence
- Your smile
- Your free spirit
- Your peace of mind
- Your power to brighten up a room by just being you

All these things and anything else you can identify as your power. All of those things are powerful. This is your power. I know you may be thinking, well, if God gave me this power how can I lose it? Easy. You ever heard that old saying, "Power isn't something you lose, it is always within you!" I agree with this statement to some degree. Yes, power is something that is always within you; your joy, confidence, peace of mind has always been in you, but I also believe as life begins to happen to you, you may encounter experiences that turn you into a person that you never thought you would be. The happiness you once had; gone. That bubbly and talkative personality that was the strength you once had? Gone. Maybe one day someone said those things that made you think at one point that you were "too much," and you decided to silence them. I know all about those feelings because that is something that I dealt with. I also believe as people come into your life there are many people who are life suckers and will drain all the power out of you if you hang around them for too long. By the time you get yourself out of that situation or even look up, you don't even recognize yourself. You one day realize your happiness, your peace of mind, and confidence is all gone.

Sometimes throughout life as life happens to you, you find yourself having less and less of your power. That is exactly what happened to me. I was walking around with not a care in the world not even realizing the power that I was carrying. I was just simply being me, not knowing that God had this power within me that others could see that I wasn't aware of. The problem with not being aware of your power, I was letting any and everything into my environment not even knowing what I carried and how powerful my power truly was. Until one day, I looked up and didn't even recognize myself. The confident, outgoing, talkative, full of peace woman was gone. I was turning into someone I no longer knew. And if I am being honest probably the first time, I even recognized that those things were even my power. Without my power I didn't feel like myself; I felt robbed. You see, I was having people who lied on me control my peace of mind. I was letting life's happenings after college control my happiness and mindset. Enough was enough, I was giving people and my experiences too much power that didn't even belong to them in the first place.

It took God to shake up things in my life for me to start snatching back my power. It took me recognizing that I had given my power up and crying out to God about how I no longer felt like me. I was drowning in this season of my life. And God had to intervene, but only by His rules.

You see, God can give you power. But if you don't recognize the things that make you powerful and stand out someone else who can see you better than you see yourself can strip you from your power if you let them. Sadly, I was a person who let certain experiences and people in my life strip me from a power that I didn't even know I had at the time.

Are you too feeling this same way? Waking up and feeling like you do not feel the same? Like if something is missing? Like a part of yourself is missing? That thing that missing is your power. There are situations that you stayed in too long. There are people that you kept around that meant you no good. And girl, if we're being honest you knew this all along. But now, you're stuck. You don't know how you are going to get back to you again after being broken from situations that broke you.

See, the good thing about God is that He knew that you would be here. He knew you would be where you are at right now and be clueless on how to get your power back. The thing about God is He wants to build you up and help you snatch back your power, but this time with Him on your side. With God on your side and you having the knowledge of the power you possess that God has given to you, you will not only be aware of the things you let around you but also you will know how to discern who to let in and who to let go in order to keep your power.

Shortly after graduating from college, I quickly realized that I no longer had any of the things that made me, me and gave me my power. I didn't have my happiness, my confidence, my peace of mind; nothing. It was as if one day I woke up and just didn't feel like myself. It was as if those situations and certain people snatched my power; or better yet, I was handing it to them little by little unknowingly. I felt weak. I felt broken. I felt alone. These feelings aren't easy to deal with. If I am being honest, I personally didn't know how to deal with them. Feelings that I never felt, but also feelings that I tried to push down because I was the "strong friend." I don't hurt like others. But the truth was I was hurting, and no one even realized. I was broken, and no one even realized. My power was gone, and I was no longer me, not even a little bit and no one even realized. That can be a hard pill to swallow when you feel like you have no one in your corner but God. It is one humbling experience. Did I feel that way when I was going through everything? Hell no. I felt the lowest I have ever felt. Nothing was happening as easy for me as it usually did. However, it was all a set up for what God was about to do in my life to build me back up stronger than I've ever been. As a Libra, (girl, what's your zodiac sign?) I do not like confrontation whatsoever, and that is exactly what it felt like to me when I had to face these feelings I was dealing with. Confrontation. If I am being honest, I was trying to run far away from that. Girl, I'm talking a full sprint from my problems, okay! Eventually I couldn't sweep my feelings under the rug any longer and keep running away from areas in my life that I needed to heal from. So, I had to be planted in an uncomfortable season. I had to go through feeling like I was alone to see who was really for me. I had to be in solitude with just me and God. I had to have God strip me of who I thought I was and rebuild me in a way that was stronger than before. I had to be in unfamiliar territory. I had to dig deep inside myself and snatch back my power from experiences that made me feel different about myself. I needed all these things to build a stronger foundation in who God was calling me to be. God was about to put me through His process in order for me to begin *Bossin' Up and Snatching Back My Power*, and the process was something that I most definitely did not prepare for. The process was hard, but I made it through with God's help, and so can you. I was being handed a mirror that was forcing me to sit up straight to face things head on. God needed me to face certain things in order for me to recognize where I had lost my power and recognize how this time, I will put up a fight and begin snatching back my power.

Is it time that you start getting your fight back to begin Bossin' Up?

I know you are facing a time right now that isn't the easiest. Maybe after college you don't feel like yourself. Or that friends are leaving you left to right. Maybe you're in a position right now that you feel that God is far away and you're all alone on this life journey called your raggedy twenties. Trust, me I get it. I was there. You are exactly where you need to be. This is where God needs you to be. He needs you at this stage to put you through His process. This fight He is about to put you in is about to show you the fight you have always had in you. Your power is yours and always has been yours, but it is up to you to get out there and begin snatching it ALL back from the things that never should've had it in the first place.

Ways to Get Your Power Back:

1. Through healing parts of you that you tucked away so deep: If you are anything like me, you buried childhood issues, current issues, hell even planned as far as the future to bury those issues. It is time you heal. It is your time. These things that you are "tucking away" or so you think are just resurfacing in ways that you are not even aware. God wants to do a new thing in you, and in order for Him to do so He needs for you to lay it all out and heal. Maybe you are wondering, well, how do I heal when I don't even know where to begin? Ask God. Trust me, He will answer you in many different ways. Maybe it will be through this book, maybe through a podcast, or casually just talking to someone that God will use to speak.

2. Being in solitude. Solitude does not mean lonely. I struggled with solitude for a bit. I confused it like everyone else with being lonely, until I realized solitude is just another way of being with self. Getting to know self on a higher level with no

distractions. It is something we all need. It was something I needed. It was a time for me to hit the reset button, pour into myself, speak to God more. Sometimes it can only be done when God has your undivided attention, and that normally is through being in solitude. God needed me at that time, and He needs you. He needed me all to Himself so I could talk to Him and rely on Him during this process. I needed His guidance more than ever. I couldn't just rely on my own understanding this time around.

3. Spend time with God, He will guide you through this process. Something I struggled with was spending time with God and at times I am not always perfect on doing it. One thing I realized is that you have to look at it like a friendship. You can't be half in or coming to God only when you need something and not ever talking to Him again until another problem arises. Talk to Him. Pick a time and spend 15-20 minutes with God. Worship. Sit in silence and let Him pour into you. He is waiting for you.

{Bossin' Up Question}

What is your power that you feel you need to snatch back?

_____
_____
_____

Who or what situation do you need to begin healing from?

_____
_____
_____

Do you struggle with spending time with God? Why?

_____
_____
_____

The Power:
Dear Self Letter

Dear Self,

Here I am questioning myself. I don't even know who I am any more. I feel lost. I feel like no one understands what I am going through. How did I lose myself? Where is my confidence? Where is my happiness? Why do I talk less? Where the hell is my power? I don't even know how to put into words what exactly it is I feel. I just know this is a feeling I no longer want to feel. How do I get back to myself? Do I even want to get back to myself? I will never forget the day that I felt all of my power was gone and not knowing really what to do because I was broken. But, let me be the first to tell you girl, you are not broken. You are stronger than you think. Yes, right now I feel broken, but I know I will rise up again. And when I do, it will be with God on my side. You are not alone. You may not have people physically in your corner, but who you do have in your corner is bigger than any person walking this earth. This needed to happen. I needed to feel powerless for a minute. I needed this build up. I needed this time for God to open my eyes wide to *work on me and build the relationship with Him. This will all make sense soon. Just hang in there Ke. Your power is coming back to you. Always remember whose you are. I love you, girl.*

PRAYER

Dear God,

Please keep me. Right now, I don't know who I am any more. I feel broken, God. I don't feel like myself. I have no one to turn to but you. I am sorry God if there were times where I neglected you. Where I didn't talk to you like I should have. I need your help. I ask that you cover me God and help me to be able to discern who needs to be around me and who doesn't while I am on this process of snatching back my power. I thank you God for putting me on this journey. I may not understand what you are doing, but I trust you God. I know that you are working everything out for my good. God, help me to snatch me back to the woman who had confidence. Help me snatch back the woman who had a positive mindset. God, help me snatch back my joy and peace of mind. I didn't recognize my power then God, but I do now. Please build me up in a way where my power can no longer be taken from me. I thank you in advance God for helping me through this journey. I ask that you help be my guide through it all even when I can't see the end result.

Amen

* *

AFFIRMATIONS:

I am powerful.
I am snatching back ALL my power.
I am on the journey to healing and I LOVE IT.
I trust God and His plan.
I am whole.
I have power over ALL THINGS.

CHAPTER 2:
The Process

"Trust the process, God is at work even in your lowest points in your life."
- Unknown

In order for God to help you on your path of Bossin' Up, you first have to be put through a process. Process can be described as a series of actions or steps taken in order to achieve a particular goal. And girl, that is exactly what God plans to do during your process. There will be a series of actions that will take place during this season. There is a series of steps you will have to do in this process. You will be faced with things you tried so desperately to bury. God will reveal who is for you and who isn't. God will also make you go through the steps of healing and facing issues head on. God has to disfigure you and mold you into alignment of what He called you to be, but first there is a process. The process is not easy, not even a little bit. God's process is hard, but very necessary. This process will help you get your fight back. The process is very important. See, if you are like me you are currently praying to God for Him to either do a new thing in you or elevate you in some kind of way. But, in order for him to do so, there are some things that God needs for you to get pruned from. So, He creates the process that will have you diggin' deep to do the inside work.

While it felt like others were out there living their best life and seeming like everything was going great for them 24/7, it felt like my life had been hit with a ton of bricks. I wasn't prepared. I wanted to do what I do best, run from all my problems instead of facing them. I quickly learned that this journey that God was about to take me on required the better version of myself; and with that better version meant that I had to do the grit work. The grit work started with me facing my issues face to face by Bossin' Up. This right here was about to be one hell of a journey.

Throughout the process you'll find that He is digging up parts of you that you have to work on. There will be things such as insecurities, past experiences, past friendships, and hurt that will be dug up during this season that God will put directly in your face and say, "here, handle that." Truth is, none of us really want to handle that and face all of our issues head on. During the season of going through God's process it is His pruning season for you. There are areas in your life right now that are broken and need healing. You need healing, even if you don't want to acknowledge it right now. God needs to get you going on working on things from the inside in order for you to begin Bossin' Up your life on the outside. The process isn't something easy, and it for damn sure isn't easy when you are in your twenty somethings. As someone who is in her early twenties, never in my wildest dreams did I think that I would be so connected to God at such an early age. Now, don't get me wrong, I grew up knowing who God was and going to church but it is a huge difference when you get to know him for yourself. Going through my own trials and tribulations I had no other choice but to get to know Him. It was through His word, through church, prayer, connecting with other people who walk and know God better than I do is where I was able to get to know Him better. Through my process in my twenties is when I got to know Him on a whole different level. There were plenty of areas that were broken in my life; but, because I played the "hide and don't seek my issues" game all my life I didn't even know how to heal from the things that I buried so deep that I one day forgot about.

In the season of God's process:

- He is going to have to break you down like never before. The break down is you being pruned from head to toe. Everything you thought was you, everything you thought you knew, and held onto will be stripped from you piece by piece. It is not in the way that you're thinking though. God does not want to break you down for you to feel weak, no. At first, at least for myself I felt

weak. I thought God was punishing me by having me tap into a part of myself, of vulnerability that I didn't know existed. Where in actuality He wants to help strengthen you in areas that may not be your strongest area right now.
- He's showing you things that may be broken in your life.
- He is keeping you isolated from everything and everyone that does not mean you well during this season in your life. He needs your undivided attention when it comes to this process

This process will make you feel like the seed you planted with the faith you had back then is now gone. I am here to tell you the seed that you planted is still there. You still have seed in you. God is just putting an extra sprinkle on this seed, that will bring about a different way for you to be sprouted and supported with sturdy foundation. God was pruning me through my season, by stripping me of what I thought I knew about my life and where I was headed. This wasn't the idea of living my best life. Instead, when I encountered the process, I ran from it. I fought God hard on it. I declined trying to live His way and wanted to do as I pleased. I didn't want to bring up old feelings and heal from things. I didn't want to actually feel my pain that I was dealing with at that current season in my life. I for sure didn't want to step into unfamiliar territory and have to leave parts of me that I knew so well behind. The feeling of having to leave parts of me that I was so used to felt like I was losing myself. I had to leave the idea of what I thought my route was going to be. I had to leave parts of people that were connected to me. I had to leave my small thinking behind; which was the hardest. God was expanding my mindset, my surroundings by preparing me while being pruned. It was a transformation that I wasn't open to at first, because it felt as though everything was falling apart, but in reality, God had a plan all along. Everything was working out for my good, I just couldn't see it yet.

Understand that though this process may not be an easy one, you are exactly where God needs you to be in this state in your life. You have tried long enough to try to fix everything all on your own, and if we are being honest it didn't get you too far. You are beginning to shed a part of you that you can no longer hold on to, and it hurts. I myself wanted to do what I do best. Run from my problems and act as if everything was fine. I guess that time for me came to an end because no matter how much I ran from this process God was like, AHT AHT. The funny thing is it doesn't matter how long you try to push the process away; it will always find its way to you. God is ready to elevate you to the next level of Bossin' Up your life. Bossin' Up in life can only be done through God's different series of steps. When I finally decided to give in and let God do His thing it was hard. The process had me questioning everything that was going on around me, it had me questioning myself, it even had me questioning God and if He was out to get me, honestly. I didn't understand the change, and when we do not understand something the first thing is question it. As crazy as it might sound, I felt that God was out to get me. I was angry with God; while it seemed as though everyone else was living their best life through social media, it felt like God was taking me through all these things just to break me down. Was He not on my side anymore? Is He punishing me? Isn't it funny how we compare our now that is happening in our lives to others on social media who may be going through the same, but through that perfect selfie you wouldn't even know?

For me, God had to break a lot of things down. If I am being honest it felt like He broke my whole life down. I felt extremely isolated from the world. I felt like I had no one to turn to when I was going through my weird stages of feeling broken. I felt alone. I felt that no one else could even be experiencing what I was going through, so it made me feel alone. How could I open up to people who think I have it all together? Will they even understand? Every part of me was being peeled back. Everything that I thought I knew about myself, God was definitely saying no, that is not you anymore. So, what I'm going to do is put you through a process. He needed me to not only heal from things, but also look within myself and unlearn any and everything that no longer served who I was. The process isn't picture worthy that's for sure. You can't just snap a quick picture and put a catchy caption for this process. It is the part you do not want to even talk about to people. You don't want to tell people about the tears you cried, the way God had to prune you, the relationships you had to let go of, the betrayal you felt, the isolation that you dealt with. Nope! You wouldn't dare showcase that, that is not for show. Why? Because we are all operating as if we are all living our best life and aren't going through anything in our twenties. Truth is, living your best life can look different in many ways. One thing's for certain is we are all going through something that can help uplift one another. This process season does not skip a soul. If you are not going through it now, just know you will one day. It may not be a season you want, but you will come out whole on the other side.

God interrupted my rhythm of how I'd seen things for myself. The process at times broke me all the way down, but I quickly realized this was a part of God's plan because the way I was being built back up was only by the way of God.

My process included:

- Dealing with certain issues in my early twenties such as post-graduate depression
- Dealing with the idea of having control over my life and letting God lead
- Taking me through a silent season where I depended on Him like never before
- God isolating me and showing who was for me and who wasn't for me
- Healing in all areas of my life that I thought I healed from: personal issues, betrayal, unforgiveness in others and myself.
- God stripping me from who I thought I was and helping guide me to my authentic self
- Remembering who the hell I am and who God called me to be. Don't get me wrong I always had a sense of who I was, and I always remained true, but there was another

level that I wasn't showing. God had to remind me the part of me I am holding back. I tapped into my higher self and realized that I am in charge of how I want this story of mine to be told. I am Bossin'. I am bad ass. I am whole, and able to walk in my power! I am powerful!

It also included:

- A lot of crying and not understanding what God was doing in my life
- Doubting myself more than ever
- Feeling alone on this journey of beginning to snatch back my power.

Was any of this easy? Hell no, but it is something that is necessary in order for you to get to all that God has for you. This Bossin' life ain't easy. You have to be willing to put a fight in order to snatch back all of your power. You have to go to war for the person that God is calling you to be. He wants more for you. He wants you to get back to you, but a hundred times better. He wants you to shine, girl. But you have to go through God's process first, and the big question is will you push through it and snatch back your power even through the confusion or will you fold?

You may be in a process season yourself and not know how to even identify it. Repeat after me: **God has me in His process. He is building me up.**

Now that we identified that you too are going through a process, you cannot fold. I want you to know that you will get through. It probably does not feel like it now; instead you feel alone, as if no one understands or can even comprehend what you may be going through. I understand, but I am here to tell you that there is light at the end of this all. This feeling you feel now is only temporary. There is a bigger picture that is trying to be shown to you. God wants you to have all of your power back; whether that be your confidence, your smile, your peace of mind, or your willingness to forgive someone easily. Through my own personal process; I snatched back my power in many ways.

I snatched back my confidence.
I snatched back my mind.
I snatched back my faith.
I snatched back my fight.
I snatched back my peace.
I snatched back the woman who let nothing come against her without a fight.
I gained knowledge from God in many ways through this all. This time when I am fighting back

to keep my power and continue to be the Boss in my life, I have God on my side.

In this season, try to avoid the "why me's" and instead ask yourself "why not me?" I know it is different to ask that question especially through God's process. But, why should He not choose you to prune you and make you whole again? You want these blessings, right? Well, He can't have you going into your winning season with the past issues haunting you because you didn't take time to handle that.

Instead, ask these questions:
What is this supposed to teach me?
Who am I supposed to become?

{Bossin' Up Questions}

What is it that God is trying to get you to face right now in your life that will cause you to begin Bossin' Up?

_____
_____
_____

In the process that God has you in right now, how are you feeling on the inside? Are you alone? Are you angry?

_____
_____
_____

If you can give yourself some encouragement through this process, what would it be?

_____
_____
_____

Understand that all of the power that you need back your way will come. However, it all starts with a process. The process feels like a storm that never ends, but like my granny says this too shall pass.

Remember: You can't want the testimony without going through the TEST.

The Process:
Dear Self Letter

Dear Self,

 This process will be a challenge, but it also isn't for the weak. God knows what He is doing, and I stand firm in that. Throughout this journey there are times where you will break down. There are times where you will wonder where God is through all this. Just know that He is with you guiding you through it all. This process is going to show you who is with you and who was never for you from the get-go. Hold on to the ones that stick through with you and build you up when you feel like your back is against the wall. This season will be full of breakdowns. You will go through a silent season, you will go through a period in your life where nothing makes sense. You will get betrayed by people that you've been loyal to. You will not feel like yourself for a quite a bit, but through this whole process of God revealing things to you, and making you face certain situations head on. He will also show you who you really are inside. He will show you the actual power you possess within you. Don't doubt this process. Yes, it may seem that others are *doing well off, even the ones that did you wrong, but this is about YOU and not about them. If God has His finger on you and trying to prune you in order to elevate you, trust you are better off in this season where nothing makes sense. Hang in there. Those tears will one day turn into your testimony. I love you, girl.*

* * *

PRAYER

Dear God,

I am angry. I am hurt. I feel betrayed. I feel like you are not on my side. Why are you putting me through a process like this? God help me to understand what you are doing. There are things in my life right now that I do not want to revisit. There are things that you want me to face right now God that I don't think I can. In this season God, help me to be open to what you are trying to do. Help me to not close up and run from my issues like I have been doing before, God. I want to be anchored in you God, and although I may be upset, hurt, betrayed, and feel like you are not near please keep reminding me that this is all you.

Amen

AFFIRMATIONS:

God is with me during this season of my life
I am trusting my process
I am beyond grateful for what God is revealing to me right now
I am stronger than I think
God is my Healer
I am already equipped to handle this process

CHAPTER 3:
20s

"Stuck in them 20 somethings. Good luck on them 20 somethings. But God bless these 20 somethings."

- SZA

Your twenties can be the hardest chapter in your life. One minute you feel like you are living your best life, and then the next minute you feel like "what the hell is going on with my life?" Well, at least that's what it feels like for me. Being in my early twenties I'm sure there are other seasoned women who would look me straight in my eyes and say, "You ain't seen nothing yet," and I am sure they're right but girl, these twenty somethings be ready to take ya girl out. As a young girl I couldn't wait to be in my twenties. I remember looking at women that were in their twenties and thinking wow they have it made, life looks great for them. I can't wait to be that age! I mean there were just so many cool things that women in their twenties could do. They could drive, drink, kiss boys and not have to answer to anyone about it, and plus the big one that we all wait for, they get to sit at the adult table! Girl, I couldn't wait to sit at the adult table and be in grown folks' conversation. Women in their twenties had it made, and I wanted to experience all of that. HA. I guess I should've listened to my granny when she would say, "Baby, don't rush to be an adult stay a kid as long as you can."

God showed me quickly that these twenties and this walk with Him wasn't about to be no walk in the park. I quickly realized the twenties I wanted to experience so badly wasn't all the way like I envisioned. Instead, I was faced with a rollercoaster ride with a whole lot of crazy twists and turns. Your twenties can be one confusing time. You envision your life going one way. The way you think all twenty something year olds are living... Fabulous! However, your twenties aren't always the case. There will be times where you are just floating through and wondering what is next. Can you relate? For most of us, it is a time where we step into the real "adult life" with no real instructions on how to navigate through. I am the first to admit I thought my twenties would be full of sparkles and just purely glamourous. Boy was I wrong! Now, don't get me wrong; in your twenties and especially in mine there are fun times, but there are also times where you have to do the grit work. I am talking real dirty. The grit work includes the side of your twenties where everyone tries to avoid. You are being held up a mirror of yourself at times and learning what are your toxic traits, and how to unlearn those same toxic behaviors. You are going through self-discovery, and at times re-self-discovery. You are also dealing with healing parts of you, all while building a relationship with God and trying to find your way back to YOU. It can be tough. It is the side that no one truly prepares you for or even gives you a manual on. Growing up, no one even displayed this part of their twenties.

At times, I never knew which direction God was going to take me. Just when I would think I was living my best life; it would feel like God snatched a rug from under my feet and directed me to a different and unfamiliar path. A path that I wholeheartedly did not want to walk on. Will you be getting off at the stop where you feel where you are living your "best life?" Or, will you be getting off at the stop where God wants to take you on a detour? We never know how this ride is going to go, but one thing for sure is that we all eventually have to get off on that stop where God is taking us. That different route than what we have actually planned for ourselves is where we have to go through The Process with God. Through Bossin' Up your life, there will be a lot of things God will reveal to you which will be identified as His Process in order for him to show you how to begin Bossin' Up your life and snatching back your power. I fought hard during this Process. I kicked, screamed, and fought God hard over this process. Guess who won? Not me, of course.

I was going to experience my first taste of The Process and here is where I began to learn how to fight back and snatch back my power:

TWENTY-ONE & DEGREED UP

May 7, 2016 was a big day for me. It was the day I was graduating from college. There I was, twenty-one and about to enter a whole new chapter in my life that I was more than ready for. Or so I thought. With my shoulder length curls flowing in the breeze, my makeup sitting perfectly on my brown skin, and my baby doll white dress hugging my petite figure, I was ready to strut across that stage and receive my degree that I worked so hard for. I couldn't contain myself as I sat there while staff members and guest speakers gave their speeches and wished us luck in our next journey. "Luck? That's definitely what I am going to need" I whispered to myself. Many people don't finish college in four years, and there I was four years later getting ready to receive my bachelor's degree. I worked hard for this. I should've been extremely proud of that, right? Well, I should've been; but what I was battling with was so much bigger. Here I am on my big day about to receive a piece of paper that basically says, girl, you are out of here, but what that paper doesn't say in fine print is good luck on finding your way. That is exactly how I felt after graduating; what is my way? Up until this point I had every internship under my belt. There was never a moment I wasn't doing something in media.

On the other hand, God has a funny way of making our realities switch gears.

After college, this new adulting life wasn't easy for me one bit. When you have your whole life after college planned out on a vision board, you can be faced with a harsh reality. My reality slapped me dead in the face. None of what I had put down had even come into manifestation. Instead, I was heading back home a couple of months after graduation with no jobs lined up. I avoided the question, "So what's next for you" like plague. I mean girl, I was from sunny ol' California where dreams come true and I just knew heading back home after college that my phone was going to be ringing off the hook. I knew I was going to land my dream job and that life was about to just be amazing for me. I had it all planned out. Regardless of what I was going through that was one thing that I was sure of. But my reality did a whole 360. I always knew what my next move was, but this time I didn't. My adulting life was beginning to look really sad, and I was honestly wondering where God was. My adult life was supposed to be amazing right? Instead, it felt like a routine. Sitting at home all day and apply to job after job. Get on social media and see everyone doing great. Meanwhile, I felt like I was being punished. Was I being punished? Did I not appreciate my past blessings enough? Did I work this hard for nothing? Here's the thing though; I didn't know it at the time but once again God didn't have those same plans. I was fresh out of college thinking I had it all planned out. With no worries I was applying to all the jobs, going to all the events and networking; I was beyond confident. You couldn't tell me anything; I just knew with this resume who can really turn me down? I mean, God wouldn't bring me this far with all this experience to leave me hanging dry right? But girl are you ready to laugh? Then BAM God was like nope, THIS is what you are about to do, not this. The joke was clearly on me. Instead of God handing everything to me that I thought I deserved; He handed me things I needed to work on which included dealing with the issues that I was running from. Isn't that crazy? Don't get me started. Here I was out of college and without a job in my field for about four months straight. When I tell you those were the longest months of my life! I was just so confused. How can I be a college graduate with a degree and literally don't have a job? I was frustrated. I was disappointed in myself. I felt like a failure. And honestly, mad at God. I started to think

God had it out for me, that he wasn't going to bless me anymore like He did in the past. I didn't want to end up like everyone else who graduated college and didn't have a job lined up for them, but here I was living that same truth. Every day I applied, and every day I got either no reply or an email saying, "Sorry, we decided to go another direction." I became depressed. I was putting the work in, why weren't things happening for me? Maybe I didn't put in all the work like I was supposed to? I would question myself. Then the real problem came when I started comparing myself to others. If He is blessing so and so why not me too? Did I not work hard enough? What is it God?! I grew angry and it showed. I was angry every day. I didn't want to go anywhere. I did not want anyone asking me anything about what I was doing at the time with my career. I don't even think my family members knew how to deal with me or even what to say as I went through this transition. The truth was, even I didn't know. I couldn't grasp that my life had panned out this way. I always heard the stories of students graduating from college and it taking them years to find a job in their field, but I just knew that wouldn't be my reality. However, it became my reality.

This wasn't supposed to happen to me. I had it all planned out, remember?

After being home for months, I had finally got a call back from a job after applying to what felt like about 1,000 jobs. I was elated! Finally! I didn't even care that it wasn't even in my field; I was just happy to get off this couch and get out there in the outside world. While I was home sitting day after day applying to jobs, and constantly hearing "we are sorry to inform you" or not hearing anything back at all, I began to fall into a depression. A post-graduate depression. A depression that many graduates don't talk about. It was the first time that I dealt with any type of depression. I didn't want to hang out with anyone. I didn't want to go anywhere. I had the most negative attitude, and all I wanted to do was lay on the couch and not have anyone talk to me. I didn't understand what was going on. I know my family was confused on why I was reacting this way. I should've been happy; I was back home, right? I wasn't though. It ran deeper than that. See, the feeling of having a routine of going to school, and having the security of internships and being praised for this or that to now nothing? It bothered me. I was holding onto my college life for dear life. I was holding onto all my accomplishments and who I was for dear life. I began to beat myself up.

Maybe I didn't work hard enough. Maybe I didn't make enough connections. Maybe I should've done this or that. And it for damn sure seemed as though everyone else who had recently graduated had their entire life together. Meanwhile, I was at home applying to every job in the book, and still not receiving a call back. It was a hard reality to face.

I went through so many emotions of being happy one minute, to feeling sad about my life not going the way I that saw it going, to feeling optimistic, to not even wanting to be bothered or move from the spot I was in all day. I wanted to just be to myself (which girl... isn't normal for my outgoing Libra self) and hide in my room all day. Life wasn't panning out the way that it should have in my eyes. I was growing angry with scrolling through social media and it seeming like everyone else was living their life like it's Golden while I sat on the couch with crumbs all on my shirt. I fell into a complete post-graduate depression. Truth was, I was really grieving that life that I thought I was going to have at the time. I was grieving the life that I had while in college. I was grieving how easier things happened for me. I felt like a failure. I ripped myself apart and pointed out all of the reasons why I am where I am in life; even though none of those things had to do with my current state. You know we tend to do that when we don't think we are where we are supposed to be. However, the reality was it didn't matter what I thought I should've done; God's plan is God's plan and no amount of hard work I put in was going to change the route He had for me. I didn't know it, but I was exactly where I needed to be.

If you too are going through this, I want you to know it will get better. It of course does not feel that way now. It can feel like God is taking you through a huge silent season and refuses to bless you but that is not the case at all. He is blessing you without you even knowing it right now. I know you are probably rolling your eyes and yelling at the book HOW? How is it gonna get better? HOW?! Trust me, I know I was the same way when people tried to feed me some positive bull when all I wanted to do was crawl in my corner and just soak in how my life sucks now. But, I am telling you it is going to get better. Because God is going to get you through it, whether that be the people in your life helping you unknowingly or knowingly, or whether that be you picking up this book to read it and follow some of my advice, you will make it to the other side.

They tell us to go to school, to get that degree, and the world is ours; but no one tells us about when the world does not become ours right after. No one tells us that sometimes what you think you are going to school for and are going to do for the rest of your life, God is somewhere on the other side saying, "AAH-AHH-AT not this route." That different route will have you feeling lost. That different route will have you questioning what did I do wrong to end up on this path? That different path will have you go through a period of your life that you wouldn't dare tell anyone. The feeling of life not happening the way you envisioned isn't fun, and the transition from college to the real world isn't easy. It's as if we got thrown out to the wilderness with no instructions on how to survive.

Sometimes that route God decides to take you on instead can be very uncomfortable and can make you feel that you are left in the wilderness with no direction.

Bossin' Tip

Dealing with life after college is never easy, and then add post-graduate depression on top of that. It can feel as though your whole life is spiraling out of control. Although many may not experience it, I need you to know that it doesn't mean that you aren't normal because you are having your own experience of post-graduate depression. It can be a heavy weight after graduating college and being pushed out into the real world. Be gentle with yourself. It is time to change your mindset. This might not be something you want to hear now but a changed mindset will change you. You are POWERFUL! The route God is taking you on may not make sense but it soon will; just hang on.

The transition wasn't a walk in the park that's for sure, and I found myself having major breakdowns every day. Girl, I am talking full on panic attacks about what is next for me. I sometimes would just cry because I wasn't as sure of my path anymore. To go from being at school where everything was centered around your passions and you were having this internship, or participated in this class that was exactly what you wanted to do in life. It is like a big slap in the face when you walk off that campus into the real world to shortly realize, this ain't it. It's as if you want to hide. I wanted to hide. Why did no one tell me about this part in your twenties? Why did no one show me that this is what you will go through after college? I sat there and judged my own path just to hop on social media and cry some more because everyone's life was popping while I was shrinking. I didn't know how to handle it. One thing is for sure, if you are going through post-graduate depression or having major breakdowns after your transition into the adulting world, you aren't crazy. We all feel these feelings, even though no one talks about it. You aren't going crazy, but what you do need to do is not compare your life to anyone else's. No matter how hard you work you can't skip the process that God has laid out for you. And boy, was I feeling that process more than ever. I probably cried more than ever at twenty-one, twenty-two, and twenty-three just trying to wrap my head around where my life is going. If you are anything like me, one thing you need to do is breathe. 1.2.3. BREATHE. Life is not a race. Yes, life might not be planning out the way you wanted to. Maybe that dream job or that dream city you thought you were going to move to right after college isn't happening, and you aren't rolling in 6 figures like you thought you should've been doing right after college. I am here to tell you, you will get through.

Your life may be spiraling out of control. I was struggling with transitioning from college to the real world. I just knew I was going to be working at my dream job; but, you need to go through this pruning season. The job you may be working at right now that is not your dream, there is something there that you need to learn first before stepping into your promised land.

You are going places, but first this season is necessary. It may hurt and be very confusing, but it is the route that God has you on. This uncomfortableness you feel is necessary. You are more than this post-graduate depression. You are more than many breakdowns you have about your life right now. I know it is difficult. I know when you look on social media and see that everyone has their dream jobs and living their best life that you look at your life and think it is total trash, but it is not. You are going through this season for a reason. Life may not be planning out the way you want it to, but what else is God trying to get you to recognize while you are in this season? For me, it was just to remind me that no matter how much I plan out my life if God wants to take a different route, best believe that route is going to be more fulfilling when I look back then the route that I tried to draw out for myself.

You have to begin Bossin' Up yourself out of this. Is it easy? No, but you can't stay stuck here forever. Yes, life didn't plan out the way you wanted it to after graduation. Yes, God is taking you on a path that is beyond frustrating. But what are you going to do about it? You can't stay stuck here forever. You are powerful. You hold the power. God has plans for you. You are entering a new level of success bigger than what you envisioned for yourself. Even if it isn't what you planned and it is uncomfortable.

How to get through with your post-graduate depression tip:

- Delete social media for a while (30-day hiatus): You don't need to be focusing on viewing anyone else's highlight reel while you're trying to get your reality together. The hiatus is worth it.
- Read a positive book that will shift your mindset
- (The book The Secret by Rhonda Byrne changed my life)
- Journal: Write to yourself what you may be going through. Get your feelings out
- (Dear Self Letters with encouragement or just truly how I felt that day always helped me get through)
- Watch positive videos that will shift your energy. (Les Brown, Lisa Nichols, Oprah Soul Sunday, Necole Kane)
- Talk to God

- Write positive sayings all around your house: Put sticky notes on mirrors. Even when you don't feel like reciting the affirmations because it feels like you are living a lie. RECITE THEM. It is helping train your brain to believe that is your reality now.

- Share Your Truth: May want to start a blog, YouTube Channel, or even a small group of recent college grads or women in their 20s. Do whatever you can do to let your truth out. You will find once you begin letting your truth out how many others have the same story.

{Bossin Question}

What route does/did God have you on after college graduation? Was it the route you predicted, or did He switch routes on you?

_____
_____
_____

Through your post graduate depression or depression in general how are you handling it?

_____
_____
_____

How do you feel God is trying to begin Bossin' you up in this particular area in your life? What power does He want you to snatch back?

_____
_____
_____

BOSSIN UP: 20s EDITION

I had finally begun winging myself out of post-graduate depression. I started realizing that I hold the power and began thinking more positive and my energy began to shift. I had made it through and somewhat began to feel like myself again. Don't get me wrong it took weeks of practicing positive talking again. It took weeks and months to dig myself out of the hole that I crawled in and became comfortable in being. But you know how the twenties are; it is full of surprises, twists, and turns. Once I thought I was done with one major hurdle in my life, here comes another surprise for me. Have you ever felt like, damn I just got through this, now God wants me to deal with some more? I was about to go through a stretching season. I thought I was being stretched enough with dealing with post-graduate depression, but of course God is like *nah, here's some more.*

God was about to take me through a season where I had to peel back the person who acted as if she had it all together and I had to deal with the things that I avoided. I was about to be in complete Bossin' Up season. A season where I had to dig deep inside of myself and heal parts of me in order for God to elevate me to the next stage in my life. In order for me to begin snatching back my power I first had to learn how to heal from past situations, forgive others, forgive myself, unlearn toxic behaviors, get my faith up, release old energy, and step into my true authentic self by shedding the old me. In this Bossin' Up season I had to be isolated; God had to do a new thing in me that He could only do with my full attention. This season of Bossin' Up in areas in your own life God is going to need your full undivided attention. He needs it to be you and Him during this time. He needs no distractions. I learned how to snatch back my power of having a positive mindset. I needed to get my mindset back. I was depressed and letting that have the power over me. Was it hard? No, I didn't even want to believe that I was going through something such as post-graduate depression. But, with me learning how to snatch back my power by snatching back my mindset with the help of God, that is exactly what helped me see my life after college differently. I began to start Bossin' Up once I realized why God was having me here even if I wanted to throw the towel in and give up on God. He didn't give up on me, and He will not give up on you.

I SNATCHED BACK MY:
Mindset

God is going to have to take you on unfamiliar territory, He will have to isolate you, and once you understand that then you will be ready to heal and snatch back your power. He is going to do a new thing in you. God is giving you your strength back, your confidence back, your fire back; everything that makes you, you. You are going to leave out of this season with all of your power snatched back, but first you have to go through a process. God's process can be tough. It's a process that will have you questioning if you are even on the right path because everything feels unfamiliar and uncomfortable. But God's process is necessary in order to begin Bossin' Up from within.

The first process for me, was being stretched.

I was about to be stretched in:

- Losing control over my future and trusting God's plans over my own
- Having to solely depend on Him to be my Provider and Healer in one of the darkest times in my life

20s:

Dear Self Letter

Dear Self,

Here I am in my twenties and it really isn't looking how I envisioned it to be. This wasn't how I thought my twenties was going to turn out. I mean, it isn't bad but this area I am in right now is just uncomfortable. I am so used to getting what I want as far as how my career is going to go. I am used to going out there and making it happen, and here I am struggling and trying to figure out what is meant for me. I am going through a depression that I don't even want to believe I am going through. I was supposed to be having this big career after college. I was supposed to be making BOSS moves but instead, God has me in a position that I am not understanding why. I did everything the right way. I went to school, I got outside experience, I created a great resume for myself and THIS is what my twenties after this degree is looking like? It feels as if God is punishing me. What am I supposed to do now? It seems as though God is blessing everyone else. Did I do something wrong? Did I not appreciate all my blessings? I am not understanding this season I am in. I am not *understanding this depression, and if I am being honest I am mad as hell. I had this vision of what my life was going to be like and now I don't even feel like God is near. Can he even hear me?*

PRAYER

Dear God,

I am hurting inside. I am suffering silently. I haven't told anyone what I am going through. This life after college is hard. Although God I try not to look to my left and right, it is hard. It seems that you are throwing blessings to everyone else and somehow all my tears and prayers are going unnoticed. I am in a deep depression God. I do not like who I am becoming and I do not know how to get out of this. Was there something I did wrong? At this point, I don't know if I am still trusting this path you are taking me on God. You promised me something than what my life looks right now. God, please just give me a sign that you are still near because right now I don't know anymore.

Amen

AFFIRMATIONS

This depression does not have a hold on me
I am more than this depression
God is lifting me out of this
I believe in myself
I believe in the power of God. He is shifting things for me right now

CHAPTER 4:
GODS PLANS VS. MY PLANS

"For I know the plans I have for you, plans to prosper you and not to harm you, plans to give you hope and a future."
- Jeremiah 29:11

God's plans can be one difficult road to follow, especially when you are going through His process. It's the process of being broken down and stripped of everything you know, to now all the plans that you had for yourself being pulled from under you as if it were a rug that you were standing on. That feeling is like no other. You sit there questioning what next? What direction should I even go in? In the year of me getting in alignment with all that God had for me, it took a lot of me having to give up the plans for my own life. Do you know how hard that is? I'm sure you do. I'm sure you have mapped out your life to the T just like me, and envisioned yourself in certain areas in your life only to find yourself in a battle. Your options are surrendering to the plans God has for your life, or to continue to operate in the plans that you have for yourself. It is hard. You spend months maybe even years mapping out on some card board of all the things you will do in life, who you will become, places you'll travel, people you will meet all for God to take you through a whole wilderness season in order to get there. Can we all say together, OH HELL NO! The thought of even having to switch careers or switch the directions that you knew for certain God was going to take you on is a lot. Having to swallow that pill felt like I was a failure. I had an idea of how my life was going to go. I was super successful in the lane that I was in at the time. I was stuck on the praise I was getting, and the voices around me telling me that I was made for what I was going for, that I felt like a complete failure if I didn't do what I thought was best. However, sometimes God will have you at a standstill labeled as a "not yet" season. There's a feeling of everything should happen now and the way you want it, and the last thing that is on your mind is patience. A lot of times, we are simply comparing our lives to others' highlight reels feeling that we should be getting blessed too. Or even that we should be much further in life than we are right now. But, one thing that I have learned is that sometimes God has to do work in you before he can unleash your YES season that you've been praying for.

The bible verse in Jeremiah 29:11 fits well, *"For I know the plans I have for you, plans to prosper you and not harm you, plans to give you hope and a future."* I didn't believe in that, feeling as though God was taking things from me and revealing other things. I personally didn't want to hear that line for the life of me. How could God want to prosper me and He has me in this season crying my eyes out and questioning my whole path? I was just doing great a year ago. What is going on? How could God say He doesn't want to harm me but here am feeling more broken than ever? How could God want to prosper but here I am going through this process that He could've gave to someone else? None of it was making sense. But the only reason why it wasn't making sense was because I was holding onto my future plans for dear life. I didn't want change in the area of my career; all I knew was interviewing celebrities on the red carpet and working in media. That is as far as I was going to go in life. I just knew I was going to be as big as Oprah, but in the media aspect, God had different plans. You see, my plans were too small. It's like that meme that you see on Instagram with the little girl holding onto the little teddy bear because she loves it. It's her comfort zone and she's crying telling God she loves it. God has his hand out with his other hand behind his back with an even bigger teddy bear saying but I have better. The little girl loved the teddy bear so much that she couldn't give it away. That is exactly how I felt about the plans I had mapped out for my life. I mean, girl, I had a whole vision board for the next 5 years; this was it. I was going to make it happen. You are most likely in the same space, holding onto what feels safe. You mapping out your own life and following the plans you set for yourself versus following what God is leading you to do. You won't always know the plans God will lead you to. Things are changing fast, and you may not be able to understand why this isn't happening, and why this is happening but one thing is you will know when God is about to take you on a different route. He will disrupt those plans you had and lead you to what He has for you. No one really wants to get off of the train they thought they were successful in. The thing is God knows how much more you are capable of. There is more that He is trying to reveal to you and show you, but first it all boils down to if you are going to surrender to His plans or are you going to continue to operate in the plans you mapped out for yourself.

Which one will it be?

I know for me, God wanted to bash my head up against the wall a couple of times, because it didn't matter how many signs He gave to me I still continued on my own path. See, God knew this is who I was, a hard headed little girl who took no direction but her own, so I mean technically is it my fault? He knew before I was formed in my mother's womb. HA. That's why I'm pretty sure God had a good laugh at me holding onto my path. He knew how I was from the beginning; He knew I would find any and every way to hold onto my plan. He knew it and this is why through God's process there were certain things that had to be shown about myself. One being, I was robbing myself of what God has for me by not surrendering to His plans. I pushed and pushed for my path, because this was my comfort zone. I was good at interviewing, I was good at this media world, I was dominating in this area. Everyone else thought so, so why should I change? You know that old saying, *"a hard head makes for a soft ass."* I was for sure about to find out what that meant because God didn't care how hard I was squeezing on to my plans He was about to switch up the game for me and that all started with me getting in Alignment with His plans.

Do you feel a sense of a tug in a different direction?

Are you fighting what God is really calling you to do because you are holding onto what is safe?

For me, I was so scared that everything God had promised or at least of what I thought He wanted for my life wasn't going to come to pass because of what it was now looking like. Better yet, I wasn't afraid of what He wouldn't do; I was more afraid of what I told Him I wanted to do that He wouldn't let come to pass. I felt like I was losing myself and this "image" I was supposed to uphold. But who was it I was trying to impress? Myself? Was I trying to impress others? It clearly wasn't to make God proud. So, he had to direct me in the right path and if that meant to stir me off the road I thought I was heading towards, then He had to do just that for me to sit down and focus.

It was time for me to get aligned. Getting aligned can be a tug a war between what you want vs. what God knows what is for you.

Year of Alignment

Entering a season where God had to show me that I was stubborn when it came to wanting to make my plans happen, I had to destroy the idea of having to be constantly on the grind. Most of us always think being on the grind means being successful, and if you aren't on your grind then what are you really doing? However, God had to show me while on this journey of learning how to release the need to control my future and realize that God is the one leading the way. I had to embrace the concept of letting Him lead. I needed to embrace the concept of not being on "boss moves" during this season. It wasn't about my career, it wasn't about being seen, this season was about my relationship with God and facing the reality of me truly not trusting in Him.

Is God trying to show you that you don't trust Him?

Are the plans you have for yourself plans that you created or is it orchestrated by God?

Have you taken the time to ask God: "God are my plans aligned with what you want me to do or am I operating from an area of fear with wanting to control my own path?"

My season of literally trusting God's plan and having to let go of my plan scared me. It was a lot of letting go of the idea I had for myself, and the reality was I was thinking too small. I began to curl back into my shell of comfort. I wanted the easier way out. I wanted my path. What God was asking me to do and be I never even thought of before. For example, writing this book. I went to school for journalism and media studies, but I thought I was only qualified to be on TV. That was my thing. I did not think I was qualified to write, especially not a book. I would say things like, "Oh no I am not a writer. I'm just good on TV." Crazy right? God saw something else in me that I didn't see in me. He already saw that I was qualified when He put the idea of me creating my own blog and sharing my truth. He already saw that I was qualified when He told me to write a book. He already saw that I was qualified when He started aligning things in my favor for me to begin my process of writing. He knew I was qualified before I even did. God started to reveal things to me and the plans He had for me by planting seeds in me. Sometimes, throughout the journey of following God's plans versus my own I stumbled on not feeling qualified. I had a hard time believing that the things God wanted me to go after that I was qualified for. How am I going to share my truths in a blog and be vulnerable to people who think I have it all together? What if they don't like it? How am I going to write a book when I don't feel like I have the best writing? God didn't care about what I thought. Without Him steering me on the path of following His plans, I wouldn't have discovered this side of myself being more than what I envisioned.

What is God trying to tell you, you are qualified for but you keep rejecting?

Are you putting something off that God told you to do?

We have all been there, especially myself; I am the Queen of putting things off even if God told me to do it. See, throughout God's process it all boils down to are you going to be disciplined and obedient to what God said?

We all have plans for our lives and the exact way they are going to go, but sometimes those plans can be way too small for where God is trying to take you. We get so comfortable with what we are good at, that when He shakes things up and puts us in uncomfortable environments. These environments force us to grow, think bigger than what we are, and we don't know how to take that in. God is trying to take you out of the small box that you keep trying to force yourself into.

Bossin' Up doesn't mean you have to be in control of everything. Sometimes you have to step aside and let God lead you to something better.

I SNATCHED BACK MY:
FAITH

God's Plans vs. My plans:
Dear Self Letter

Dear Self,

God is about to switch it up on you. You are so used to having your plans set in stone and not really including God in the plans. That is all about to change and you are about to flip. Here is the season where God has to show you that you need to lose your control, and trust Him. Your issue is that you trust your own my plans over God's Plans. You need the feeling of not having it all together or not knowing what is next. It is time to let go of the idea of having it all together. God is going to sit you down for a while, and it will be hard at first, but you will eventually give in and let God have His way. Let go and release of wanting to have control. This may be hard for you, but you will make it through. I love you, girl.

PRAYER

Dear God,

I want to thank you for this switch. I did not recognize the stubbornness I had with you when it came to my future. I was trying to control my life and not even consult you in it. Please forgive me for that God. I ask that you keep guiding me on the path that you want me to be on. Help me to have the discipline and obedience when you instruct me on what it is you want for me.

Amen

* *

AFFIRMATIONS

God's path is way better.
I trust God and the journey He is taking me on.
I am walking into my purpose with confidence.
I have unshakable faith.

CHAPTER 5: SILENT SEASON

"Before anything great is achieved, your comfort zone must be disturbed."

- Ray Lewis

My first assignment of being stretched was going through a silent season. This was a season where I felt as though my growth with God, my mindset, my faith, and being content with where I was, was being stretched in order for me to get in alignment with what God was trying to do in me. God had been disrupting my silent season while I've been on this journey, but this season was on a whole other level. This silent season forced me to see things about myself that I needed to change. This silent season I was able to see that I needed to be stripped bare. I had to be stripped of the career that I thought I was going to have straight out of college. I had to be without a job for a while to be reminded by God that He was my provider. I had to be stripped on my dependency of creating my own way and letting God lead the way even if the route seemed a little all over the place. I had to be stripped from relationships that I was holding onto. All of this was beginning to happen in my silent season, and I honestly didn't know how to handle it all at once. There were times that the only thing I could do was cry out to God in this season. I'm talking tears all over my face screaming at God. I was more angry than anything. I saw this silent season as punishment. I couldn't hear his voice. *Maybe He doesn't care?* I would often think.

It was as if everything was going wrong in my life and nothing was going right. I finally got a job after receiving that degree and had managed to be there for a good six months feeling good about it. That is, until God instructed me to go a different route. Do you know how confusing and frustrating that can be? I was without a job for a good few months straight after college, and now God was having them switch up again after having a steady income. This can't be life. I had begun to feel a little down about the new route God was taking me, especially because I was enjoying the direction I was on even though I knew there wasn't any growth in it. Isn't it crazy how we will stay in something even though we know that growth is no longer attached to it? In my case I was attached to the money I was making. I vowed to myself I would never feel as broke or feel low as I did after I graduated college. So, I was willing to hang onto anything even though God was directing me elsewhere. God told me after praying to him with a clear answer to quit something I was attached to. As scared as I was, I was obedient. Soon, the fear began to kick in that I will be back to square one. No money, no job, and that depression kicking in once all over again? I couldn't have that. No way. I couldn't feel that feeling again. So, what did I do? I went out and found a job. I was determined, but this time I didn't include God in the mix. I was trying so bad to never feel the feeling that I was willing to risk not being in alignment just to make sure I had money in my pocket. I scored an interview with a company, with higher pay which I was so happy about, and they wanted to hire me and come back in next week to do the paperwork. I was beyond excited! The anxiety I had towards slipping back into what I was dealing with months back wasn't about to happen. I can now breathe. It was all working out.

The funny thing about God is, He finds our simple plans humorous.

Weeks had rolled by and I was calling the job seeing why haven't I heard back from them. I sent emails, and heard nothing back from the company! I thought it was the weirdest thing. *I was perfect in the interview, like I know for a fact they loved me.* I had so much hope in this job. I had a backup plan, or so I thought. I had some confidence that God was just blocking me because maybe it wasn't a good fit for me. Maybe God had something better lined and I was thinking too small. More weeks had rolled by and still nothing, the money I had saved up began to dwindle down. I was in full panic mode. I couldn't go back to how I was a few months ago. Doesn't God know this?!

Little did I know God knew that the jobs that I was applying for, going on interviews for, and feeling hopeful for were not a good look for me. Instead, God saw fit for me to be stretched in this season. The season of no job, wondering how I was going to make money or pay for things, God saw fit for me to go through a process instead. I was angry. I didn't want to go through a silent season. I wanted a good paying job.

BOSSIN' UP:
PHASE ONE OF BEGINNING TO SNATCH BACK MY (YOUR) POWER:

Being Stretched

God's plan of me being stretched in my faith, my character, and knowing who really is my provider was the best job I had during my silent season. It helped me level up. It helped to begin Bossin Up my faith. The phase of me beginning to snatch back my power had all started with me having to be stretched by God first. Not only was I dealing with figuring out my twenties and the crazy twist and turns I was going through, but now I was entering this silent season where I had no job, and no income coming in. All I had at the time was to lean on God, family, and have a clear understanding of who was for me and who wasn't. I had to develop faith. God was opening my eyes to so much during my silent season. Did I notice it first? Hell, no. I was completely lost. It was hard to have faith in something and in this season of my life when nothing was making sense. I can remember times I would cry to some of my close friends about what I was going through and they let me have my moment, but also quickly reminded me that I need to Boss Up. I didn't want to hear it though. I saw this stretch as just wicked. How could God do this to me again? Is this a sick game, give me a job, tell me to quit, to be right in the same situation?

The crazy thing though I wasn't in the same situation. God was about to prepare me for this. This silent season that I saw as punishment was about to bless me in many ways that I wasn't even prepared for. This was the stretch that I needed. This silent season helped me lay out all of my worries, dreams, fears, insecurities before God because I mean, on days where I should've been at work it was just me and Him. I spent days getting into the Word more. Watching sermons, and just simply talking to Him out loud. During this silent season He is shaking up your comfort zone. Your comfort zone is being disturbed which is forcing you to begin Bossin' Up in all areas in your life. The big key to Bossin' Up your life is dealing with the part where God is going to stretch you, and that is exactly what God was doing in my life. And the first part to being disturbed is to be stretched. There were days I felt completely whole during this season and there were days that I felt myself slipping back into the woe is me mentality. Being stretched in Silent seasons aren't easy. In order to get in alignment with what God is doing in your life, this is a step that cannot be skipped. I felt forgotten. The truth was God did not forget about me in my silent season, and God hasn't forgotten about you. This season is here to help you even though it feels like hell at the time. My silent season was for me to see things in myself. Things that God needed me to be aware of in order to fix. It was for me to get closer to God, and that is exactly what He wants for you. Yes, the season hurts but it is time you start Bossin' Up in your faith and trust in Him. I am sure you can relate; during this season of being stretched I am sure you feel alone. I am sure you feel like God is taking you through a maze that doesn't make sense now. I am sure you feel as though you cannot share your truth with anyone else, because I mean who will understand? Silent seasons are not something that we automatically jump for joy for. It's a season that makes you question everything. It makes you question God. It makes you question yourself. It makes you question life. It's like damn I got all these questions and God ain't sending not even one answer? Truth is He is sending answers during this difficult season, but because your thoughts are clouded with what is going wrong and what isn't going right in your life that you don't see this silent season as a blessing. You being stretched right now is your first sign that God is on your side. God needs you in a shift, He needs you to be uncomfortable and be pushed out of your comfort zone. God needs your full attention.

I know you may be going through a silent season and being stretched in the most uncomfortable way. Your faith is being tested. It all feels unfamiliar and to be quite honest it is unfamiliar. God is doing a new thing in you. See, you are different. This path God is taking you on is to make you shine bright but you can't shine bright without getting cleaned off first. And that is what God is doing, cleaning you right up. But, in order for you to hear and understand what is going on you first need to shift. So everything that you thought you knew about yourself, and the way you thought your life was going to pan out will all switch in the stretched season. It will feel like punishment. It will feel like God is hiding you at a time where you feel that you should be out there living your best life. The thing is He is making you greater while he's hiding you. He is doing the work behind the scene. This season is to make you grow, and you can't grow without being stretched. It is not a season that is the easiest and at times you will not even understand. God has to stretch you, and in order for Him to stretch you He has to check you. You will want to throw the towel in, but don't. There is not only growth on the other side, but wisdom and a connection with God like never before. There is a new you, with a powerful mindset through this shift.

As my silent season continued, I was being stretched into solitude where it really was just me and God and two solid friends in my corner. God was isolating me from a lot of people during my silent season. It was a time that I needed to really have no one around me that wasn't in alignment with what God was doing in my life; and that meant getting rid of people. It hurt like hell. I didn't feel that it was necessary in the beginning. I wanted God to do a new thing in me, but I also wanted Him to let me keep the people I wanted around. Even if I knew that didn't mean me any good. Don't we always want God to do a new thing, but also let us still keep what feels like comfort? Unfortunately, it does not work that way. I had started to believe something was wrong with me and who I was as a person when relationships ended. I was feeling like people were dropping left to right in my life. The reality was God needed for those people to walk away. God can't do a new thing in you still surrounding yourself with what He needs for you to let go of. He needed those people to show their true colors and for me to cut ties. He couldn't do a new thing in me or show me what He needed to if I held on. And boy, did I hold on until I couldn't hold anymore. During the season of being stretched there will be people that walk away from you, there will be people that you thought were going to be in your life forever, your Ace Boon Coon that you have to let go of, there will be people that show their true colors during your silent season. There will even be people that won't understand the transition you are going through, and will go as far as to question why you are changing. You are changing, and it is okay. You are becoming everything that God has called you to be. He is leveling you up to begin Bossin' Up your life in all areas and that includes having people around you who are on this Bossin' Up journey as well. He can't do a new thing such as stretching you if you have things around you that don't align. If we are being honest, it hurts, it hurts for damn sure. You can't wrap your head around why you are going through a season such as this. Now God is taking people and things away from you during the whole process? *Why? Why do you have to be the one that loses people? I know you're thinking I'm a good person. Why am I going through this?* I thought these same thoughts. I was really losing it. I felt like I was losing myself. If God wanted people to stretch and take through a season of growth I mean, there were so many people I could've named dropped for him if he wanted to stretch someone. But me? Why?

The truth was, I wasn't losing myself and God wasn't punishing me. I was beginning to come into alignment with the blessings God was trying to give me, but first the cleanup had to begin.

Here I was not only questioning where my twenties were headed and my career while God was stripping me from that, but now God is forcing me into alignment that He has for me, and taking people from me along the way? Do you know how that feels? To go from someone who is outgoing and having so many friends to feeling that everyone has turned against you during this time and you are alone? It was a season I wouldn't even wish on my worst enemy. It was a season that I questioned a lot. I questioned everything. My silent season I had to let go of the idea of how I had my life planned out. I had to let go of where I was supposed to be in my twenties. I didn't only have God stripping me of the path I was depending on, but He was also making it a point to stretch me in my faith. Stretching me in my connection with Him, and stretching me in my character. He was stretching me so much that anything that didn't align with my purpose was being pulled away. It was all a process. The stretching needed to happen in order for me to even think about snatching back my power. It may seem as though people are falling from left to right, it may seem that during this process that you feel alone and don't even know where you went wrong. Trust me, I know all about those feelings. Days you may want to throw the towel in and really go head to head with God because this is not what you had planned. But, God needs to change things up for you to realize where your power left. He needs to show you how to get that power back, and what better way than to do it in a season where you have to grow in Him? Where you have no one to lean on but Him? Where you are isolated from all people and distractions so you can hear Him clearly? I needed my power back, but in order for me to have that power again, my mindset and environment was going to have to change. The environment that I thought was serving me, was no longer. It was a shift that was taking place, and the first shift was handling the stretch in having to snatch back my mindset. Shifting your mindset to see your silent season as a blessing is how you will snatch your power back. You are going to have to connect with God like never before. It will take all of you and God to not look at your situation of a silent season as a curse or as something negative. It took me awhile to grasp that. I personally didn't like change that much, especially when it wasn't something that I planned for. The funny thing is, even though your silent season feels like hell and you may be questioning what is going on in your world right now, you prayed for this moment. You know how you want to be successful? You know how you want that better paying job? Or whatever you may have asked for, he is giving you just that and bigger but first this shift has to take place. This silent season where it is just you and Him has to take place. He needs to break you down and build you back up whole with Him on your side. This time you won't fold. This time your power can't be taken from you because you know whose you belong to.

That was when I was being put to the test. The stretch first started with me shifting my mindset. I always looked at myself as someone who had pretty great mindset. Always thought positive about my future, very optimistic, and there was rarely a time where I was scared to step out on faith. Until, I faced a silent season. Everything wasn't being handed to me easily like it used to be. I didn't know how to deal. My mindset began to become very negative. I didn't believe in my future anymore, and thought this was the end of me. I was through. Little did I know, this is exactly where God needed me. He needed me to feel this way, because in the past I wasn't really operating on faith; I was more so operating from a place of security. I felt safe as long as I made the plans for my life, so it was easy for me to go after those things. God needed me to sit down to show me in this silent season how weak my faith really was. My mindset wasn't operating in the highest frequency I began to settle on an average life. I was fine with making whatever income and accepting that the dreams I had would not come to pass. God was helping me recognize that it is not that my dreams are not going to come to pass, but that I let my power go in the process. You may be in the same place; you feel that the journey you thought you knew you were going to have is no longer going to happen because God has you in a position that is uncomfortable and unfamiliar. You feel as though you no longer have faith in anything, and that God forgot about you. Maybe you think you are not worthy any more of what you thought you were once so hype over happening in your life. It is a lie! That is a lie. Your mind is playing tricks on you, and God needs you to recognize in this silent season how to get your fight back. He needs you to recognize that yes, you may be lacking faith now but in this silent season he is going to stretch you in the area of your faith so you can snatch back your number one power: Your mindset.

My power was my mindset, and I needed to snatch it back because where it was heading wasn't even who I was. I had to quickly realize that I am exactly where I am supposed to be. You are exactly where you need to be. The silent season makes you feel alone. It feels as though no one else in this world could be possibly going through what you may be going through. That stretch was necessary; God needed me to feel the way I was feeling. He needed me to be in that situation. During the season of being stretched in my faith, alignment, and my dependency with God I began to transform. I began to become real with myself and how I truly felt in this season. I talked to God more about my frustrations. I told God the negative thoughts I was fighting. I told God I was doubtful of myself and where my future was heading. But most importantly, I made it a point through all the uncertainty to ask God to guide me during this season. I knew I didn't feel like me, and I knew this isn't who God was calling me to be. Some weak girl who doubts everything? Nah. God created me for more. He created me to be a game changer, and how am I going to do that with giving my main power away? So, I sought Him during one of the hardest times of my life. One thing you need to know in this silent season that I wish I had someone tell me is that God isn't punishing you. That through all of what you may be feeling inside and yes, it may be full of uncertainty, doubting yourself, over analyzing everything (take it from a Libra I know all about it, girl) and simply okay with playing small because things are beginning to be tough. I am here to tell you are not weak. You are not someone created to doubt yourself and feel as though you are not worthy. You are worthy, you are beyond worthy or God wouldn't have you in this season. You are more special than you know. God knows, and it's time that you know that this silent season is exactly where you need to be. This is the shift you asked for and it's happening. Just in a different way than you thought. You know that dream job you want or the success you keep envisioning it will come to pass? Well, it's happening but the seed is going to be planted first, and the seed must grow. In order for it to grow God has to keep watering you in areas where you will begin to see the growth. You are blossoming, but first this silent season is what you must face. God needs to be sure that you develop a relationship with Him before He hands out your blessing, and what better way than having you call on Him during a silent season. He needs for you to feel what it is you are feeling and go through this process of solitude. You feel everyone left you and you are angry about it? It's okay, He's stretching you. You feel upset because God has you in a position where you aren't making any income during a time where you need to be? It's okay, He's stretching you in your faith. You feel alone because you feel that everyone else is living their best life and there isn't any way that someone else can be going through what you are going through? You feel angry at God because He is making you go through it? It's okay, He's stretching you to form a better relationship with Him during it all. He needs you to be unsure in your path, so He can be sure to be the one to put the confidence back in you. He needs you to doubt yourself, so He can be sure that when He begins shifting your mindset that you know you have the power to snatch back your mindset, because you have Him helping you fight the fight. He needs to show you step by step on how to begin Bossin' Up your life, and that begins with seeing areas in yourself where you are weak. This silent season is exactly what you need.

Your Power - Your Mindset
How to snatch back your power:

- Seeing the season you are going through in a positive light. Get up every day and shift your mindset by saying something positive about your situation. *Ex: God is shifting my season as we speak for my good*
- Meditate for 5 minutes (find a 5 min meditation on YouTube. Before picking up your phone to scroll through social media, take time to begin your day feeling leveled)
- Write your feelings out
- Talk to God about your true frustrations. See God as one of your best friends and don't be afraid to let Him know the way you feel in this silent season.
- Watch positive videos to shift your mindset (even if you do not feel like it). Be aware of what feeds your mind, cut out anything that is not feeding positivity; including music and what you watch
- KEEP A SOLID CIRCLE. This will be the time that God reveals to you who is for you

when you are at the lowest point. Your circle will be the ones that keep you lifted when you feel you are slipping at times

What is it that God is trying to reveal to you about where you are at in your silent season?

Do you need to snatch back your mindset?

Do you need to begin Bossin' Up in your faith?

Write down 3 things you may be facing in a silent season:

_____
_____
_____

How is your silent season making you feel? Do you feel God is punishing you?

_____
_____
_____

What have you learned so far in your silent season? Have you realized that you are weak in some areas and need God to help you begin snatching back you power?

_____
_____
_____

In my own silent season of being stretched, God was showing me:

1. That I needed to depend on Him more and not only have faith in Him when things were going as planned, but to have faith in him when things were all falling apart. UNSHAKABLE FAITH!
2. Who was really there for me and encouraging me even in my lowest points
3. Helping me realize that my relationship with Him was weak and I needed to get into the Word more.
4. No matter how much I had my life "mapped out," I needed to learn that God will change the route at any given time and I needed to be okay with things not going as planned.
5. Find peace with where I may be in life at the moment (even if it's not what I pictured).
6. He will still provide in your silent seasons.

I SNATCHED BACK MY: **MIND**
I SNATCHED BACK MY: **PEACE**

My silent season humbled me. It made me realize that a silent season isn't there to punish me; it was a place that I needed to be. I needed the connection with God in order for me to realize things in myself, and work on those things. It forced me to begin pulling back layers of myself and work on things God was pointing out when I had no distractions. He is doing the same for you in your own silent season all while building something new in you.

Silent Season:
Dear Self Letter

Dear Self,

    This season in my life almost broke me. This silent season right now will feel like your lowest point in your life. There will be a lot of tears shed, there will be a lot praying, there will be times that you get fired from a job, there will be times where you will not be working for a while. But, through it all trust God. There is a reason why you are here. In this silent season, God needs you still. You are always on the move. He needs you still for Him to talk to you. He needs your undivided attention. In this season yes, you will feel broken, and alone, but God is about to restore you in so many ways. Your healing is coming. Your peace is coming. This is when you will be able to see the miracles that God is able to do in your life. Your mindset will be strengthened. You will have the right people around you helping you through this season. This season is launching you off into the season of abundance. Hang in there. Love you, girl.

Prayer

Father God, please cover me and my mindset. I know that you have me in this season for a reason. I know this is all a part of your process. I know there are things that I need to strengthen, one being my mindset. I know that you wouldn't call me to a silent season if it wasn't necessary. But, if I can be honest God this season hurts. I do not understand it. I feel lost. I feel alone. I feel punished. I am angry. This is a season that at times fight to understand, God. But, I trust you. I need you to cover me God through this shift. I need you to clear my mindset and help me to know how to put up a fight when negative thoughts creep in God. Download the wisdom I need to know in order for me to begin Bossin Up and snatching back my power during this silent season. And forgive me God, if during this process I second guessed what you can do in my life. Forgive me if at times I'd rather soak in everything that's going wrong and not recognizing the importance of this process. I may not understand now, but I know you will not lead me into the wilderness without equipping me with the knowledge to fight this process. Help me to not only see the positive in all this God, but for me to walk away from this silent season with a whole new outlook of my journey. I thank you God in advance.

- Amen

Affirmations:

I am bigger than where I am right now in life.
God is doing a new thing in me.
This is all working out for my good.
I am snatching back my mindset.
I am coming out whole with God on my side.
This silent season is setting me up to win.

CHAPTER 6:
Frenemies

"Circle got smaller, everybody can't go."
- Nipsey Hussle

You will quickly learn in the season of solitude with God that everybody can't go, including friends. It is a reality check that stings the most. Especially when you have an idea in your head of who you wanted to share experiences with, share successful moments with, and just share overall special moments in your life with, that you thought would be in your life forever. However, when God is pulling the plug on something that you need to let go of, He will begin exposing you to the true character of others surrounding you.

"People will always reveal themselves when you are low and down. This is the part in your process when you will realize everybody can't go. It will hurt as hell. Friendships are like intimate relationships, and sometimes it can hurt way more when you end a relationship with a longtime friend, but God knows what He is doing."

There's this saying that my granny used to always tell me, "Some people come into your life for a reason, a season, or a lifetime. It's you who has to determine what role they play."

My grandma's saying reminded me of a sermon I came across in college on YouTube. In the series Bishop T.D. Jakes preached a segment called,

"Beware of Three Types of Friends." It breaks down the three types of people you will interact with throughout your journey to your destiny. They are your constituents, comrades, or confidants. In other words, they are your reason, season, or lifetime type of people. You won't always know right away how to determine where these people stand in your life. But, a shift will eventually take place in your life that will give you a front row seat that reveals the true character of people. Character never lies, pay close attention.

As a person's true character is revealed to you, you will discover that person to either be a constituent, comrade, or confidant. A constituent is someone who is there for their own purpose. They aren't here for you; they are into what you are for. So, as long as you can get them to where they are going, they are here. But, as soon as they find someone who can further their agenda and help them get to where they need to faster, it's to hell with you (reason). A comrade is someone who is not for you, nor are they what you are for. Comrades are simply against what you are against. They come around and team up with you in the moment of battle because they too are against that, but once that's accomplished their temporary motive ends (season). Lastly, there's your confidants, these are people that are for you, are into you, whether you are right or wrong, up or down. Your confidants are your people you can lay your trust in. They are in it for the long-haul (lifetime).

As you begin elevating in life, you will figure out within your circle what roles people are playing. It's a process that I personally dread. I've always had a difficult time with recognizing who was for me and who wasn't for me, just because how I operate and how I know I wouldn't do people the way they do me. I quickly learned that just because you operate one way in a friendship, does not mean others may. Don't be fooled with thinking that people have the same heart as you. There will be times where God will reveal not only things about yourself, but He will reveal who is around you, and it is up to you to begin choosing you. Your life is like your own business. You are the CEO of it. You have the power to remove people who drain you, and the power to keep people who vibrate higher with you. There will be many times throughout your journey where you will have to eliminate and promote people in your life. It's all a part of the process. Your soul tribe (confidants) will eventually appear, but don't fear the process of solitude as you figure out what people's true roles are in your life.

One of the hardest things to deal with is a frenemy, because you view them as a friend, but secretly they're your enemy. The tricky part is you really don't know they're an enemy until a situation happens that exposes their true feelings. I went through a period where I was betrayed and made out to be this person that I was not. I had to deal with that silently. That betrayal felt like a jab to who I was as a person, who I was as a friend. I didn't know how to process it all. During my process of having to deal with being betrayed I felt broken. I felt like I was dealing with everything silently, and I didn't know who to turn to. The anger I felt, the hurt I felt, the loneliness I felt was something I wouldn't wish on my anyone. The damage after betrayal is real, and for a while I couldn't see past it. Betrayal can be one of the worst feelings ever. You suffer alone and quietly try to put the pieces together wondering, why would they do this? I've been so loyal to them, why me? How did I not see this coming? You're hurting like hell, you are angry, you want answers, you are confused, and you don't know who to trust. The worst part about it all, is you have to sit in the betrayal and silently deal with it, while the ones who betrayed you move on as if nothing had happened.

Isolation

During my time of feeling all emotions of anger, hurt, loneliness I felt isolated. I felt the loneliness I've never felt and that no one was riding out for me like I ride for them. Do you know how that feels? It can be one of the worst pains to deal with. I struggled with the idea of if I was the one who was a bad friend. Maybe I was the issue? God soon revealed to me that that wasn't the case. He showed me through confirmations through people who reminded me what type of person and friend I was. He reminded me when He let me know how He sees me. Although, I felt isolated and alone, I really wasn't. God was with me. It was just me and God. I mean, that part wasn't bad, but I am used to being a person of many friends. So when God stripped me from all I knew and made it just be me and Him, for a while it was hard to adjust. During the time of me dealing with God healing me, there were plenty of times where I felt like I was missing out. There were plenty of times where I felt broken. There were plenty of times where I just felt so alone that I was willing to make things work instead of listening to what God was telling me what was best, and that was let go of certain people who meant me no good. You will go through the same feelings. It will be hard. You will feel that you are "out of the circle," whatever that means. But, let me be the first to tell you, YOU are the circle. Your loyalty, the type of friend you are, the good heart you have will take you far. It may not feel like it right now. You may feel betrayed and may feel that God is putting you through some unfair things right now during the season of feeling isolated. However, it is necessary. God may need you to take a look at yourself. Maybe in your next friendship the ones that are sent to you by God, He wants you to do things differently. Although I consider myself a damn good friend, there are things I noticed I can work on when I was going through my own process.

Things I will do differently in my circle from God:

1. Communicate: Just like any relationship you have to communicate. Some of us only think that needs to happen in a romantic relationship. Nope! It can be with your friends as well. When situations arise speak up about it. In love, of course.
2. Awareness: When people show you who they are, BELIEVE them the first time. Do not try to hold onto a friendship/relationship that is beyond toxic.

3. Boundaries: Just like any relationship there has to be boundaries set and it has to be respected from both ends. God showed me that this was something that I struggled with in all relationships, and it was something that I needed to do differently.
4. Being Clear: Being clear on who I am. Who I want around me, and not accepting anything less.

Sometimes you have to step back and ask yourself, what can I change as well for me to be a better friend?

Betrayal working in your favor.

In this season of God exposing you to yourself, He will also expose people who are disguised as your friends. God has to expose character and motives. He needs to show you who is for you and who is not for you before he takes you to the next level in Bossin' Up your life. This process was one of the hardest for me. God not only stripped me of who I used to be, but also exposed certain relationships and showed me how weak the actual bond was. He showed me in many ways that I thought were unfair at the time. He caused issues to happen in personal relationships and showed me face to face how certain people really felt about me within the relationship. He gave me a clear picture. A front row seat. In order to even strip me of the traits I was picking up He needed to show me who I was surrounding myself with, and their true character. Once God gave me that eye opener, I knew that wasn't who I wanted to be like. So, I had to be stripped of who I was used to being. God made sure to strip me and expose each and every relationship that meant me no good. I felt like I was being hit from left to right on this process. I would sit and ask God why wasn't He aligning me with people who matched my loyalty? What was I doing wrong? It became a pity party and it became one fast.

I soon began realizing that sometimes God will put betrayal in your life to give you that push you need. That's exactly what that betrayal did; it gave me the push I needed. I started to shake off the woe-is-me attitude and I began seeing the positive in the betrayal. Those frenemies had an agenda the whole time, but God was about to turn the betrayal around for my good.

I've learned there are two ways you can look at betrayal. You can either see it as a good thing and flip it into something positive, or you can see betrayal as a negative thing, and sit with the situation. The choice is yours. I chose to flip it. When I flipped it to see the positive, that is when the betrayal started to work in my favor. The ways they worked were:

1. It brought me closer to God.

During the time of feeling alone and knowing the truth of how everything went down, the only person I had to lean on, was God. The only person that I could express all of my hurt to was God.

2. Healing, peace, and happiness.

During this process I was only looking to heal myself from this situation alone. Once I started to heal from this one situation, I started to look at other situations that happened in my life. I didn't think I needed healing from them, there I was healing from that too. Within my healing process I also started to make peace with the betrayal, and I peacefully detached from those who had hurt me. I took time to work on me. I started to feel this peace and happiness come over me.

1. Brought out the BOSSIN beast in me.

I became a beast and not in a negative way. The betrayal started to stir me in the right direction and made me want to stand in my TRUE authentic self! It made me want to start Bossin my life. I was no longer afraid to say this is me, you like it or you leave it. I was no longer afraid to cut ties from the wrong people. I wasn't afraid to speak up if someone did me wrong. I was Bossin' my way back to being me!

2. Pushed to step into my purpose.

Believe it or not, the betrayal pushed me into what I believe is my purpose. I believe it is to share my story with others and help others heal. And that's where my blog Bossin' Her 20s was created from. From that hurt and betrayal. It initially was a way for me to heal myself but, eventually I started sharing my stories with others and receiving messages that my blog posts have been helping them heal and deal with the same situations.

So in a sense, I was blessed by the betrayal. I didn't know that at the time, and it sure as hell didn't feel like it. Once I started to see the blessing in the betrayal, that is when everything started to align in my life. If the betrayal didn't come, I wouldn't have started working on me and becoming the best version of myself. If the betrayal didn't come God wouldn't have been able to show and release the blessings that he was trying to show me all along, but couldn't until I got from around the wrong people. If betrayal didn't come, I wouldn't have formed the close relationship with God that I have now. If betrayal didn't come, I wouldn't be walking in my purpose. That betrayal did more than hurt me, it made me find me again, the authentic me. And from that point on, my life began to change for the better. It worked in my favor.

Betrayal of course can hurt. Having someone who you've been loyal to turn their back on you, hurts. But there has to be a switch in all of it. You have to take that betrayal and spin it in your favor.

Ask yourself: How can this betrayal work in my favor?
What did I learn from this betrayal?

Don't allow what someone did to you continue to shape and change your life in a negative way. Instead, spin that situation and use it for your good. Allow that betrayal to make you look deep inside of you, and ask yourself what needs to be changed? What did I learn from that season with the friendship? What do I see in myself that I too need to change?

I SNATCHED BACK MY: **VOICE.**
I SNATCHED BACK ME!

Frenemies:
Dear Self Letter

Dear Self,

This place you are in right now will not last. God is going to soon give you the peace in your healing that you need. The way you feel is valid. The way they did you is wrong. You have every right to feel the way you feel. It is okay to acknowledge that you are hurt. You don't always want to be positive, sometimes you want that revenge. You are having a hard time with healing from this, but let me tell you God is on your side on this, even if it does not feel like it. This betrayal needed to happen in your life. It showed you many things. This betrayal not only showed you who was for you and who wasn't, but it showed you the power that you have within yourself. This betrayal was also a wakeup call for you with recognizing you were letting others have too much power over you. It showed you to be mindful of the energy you keep around you, and to always protect you. This betrayal woke up a beast. You won. No, not in the petty way but because you chose you. You recognized that the relationship that turned on you was right on time. The same people that thought they were "cutting you off," don't even know the blessing behind that. The real blessing is that God is weeding out the friendships that can no longer serve you. He is getting ready to place you in an environment that can pour into you and you can reciprocate that same energy. It will hurt. It will sting. It will feel lonely, and feel as though everyone turned their backs on you. Trust, it's better for God to reveal who your frenemies are now in this season rather than later on. Yes, you are hurt. Yes, you wish things can go back to the old times. But, you also recognize that even if they don't, you are okay and at peace. At times you feel like you are being punished; why is God taking people from you? You are not. There are reasons, and maybe just those people were never for you. Maybe your season and their season in your life ended. Keep being who you are and just know God is sending your tribe. I love you, girl.

PRAYER:

Dear God,

Thank you for revealing people's true characters. Although my feelings are hurt for many reasons, I want to thank you. I know there is a bigger picture and one day it will be revealed to me. I thank you God that during this you are helping me to see the positive in it all even if I still am dealing with the feelings of being betrayed. I thank you God for working on the inside of me and bettering me before sending me my tribe. I thank you in advance God for the tribe you are sending my way.

Amen

AFFIRMATIONS:

I am a good friend.
My tribe is finding its way to me.
I am snatching back ME through all of this.
I am more than worthy to have good people around me.

CHAPTER 7:
Healing 101

"I wanted revenge, but God gave me peace."
- Unknown

Healing from the past is one of the hardest things to do. You can move on in life and grow, but past situations that haven't been dealt with will always find a way to creep back up in your mind. Certain experiences that you may have happened in the past can leave you angry, hurt, and frustrated to the point where you hold onto every detail. This eventually robs you from your true happiness. The biggest test that God gave me during my process was healing. Like I said in the beginning of the book, God put a mirror right in my face and made me dig deep. Diggin' deep also came with having to heal, and it just wasn't one level to healing. It felt like a billion levels. Just when you think *okay I am healed now I'm happy* here comes more feelings that makes you think otherwise. The healing process that no one talks about is hard. It's easy to say that you forgive others or that you moved on, but the real question is, have you really?

I would find myself moving on from people or situations, but the hurt that happened in between I would still hold on to. I did a lot of replaying situations over and over and over again. I would get furious with the thought of I should've done this, I could've said this, and the list goes on. I wasn't even realizing that I was doing way more damage to myself by replaying these situations every chance that I got. I wanted to be free from the hurt that I felt from the past. I wanted to shake off those memories and just be happy. But it didn't happen overnight.

Are you in a place where you know you need healing?

Is there something that still bothers you to this day as if it happened yesterday?

If you answered yes to either one of those questions it is time that you heal. I am proud of you for recognizing that you need to heal, but the difficult part is actually putting in that action. In order for God to do a new thing in you and help you on this Bossin' journey, you can't take your 1937 resentment and walk into your blessing. That is why He has you where He has you. You may feel stagnant or feel like you are carrying a lot. It's because things need to be released and some of those things start with healing. There is no way he can bless you without killing your flesh of unforgiveness.

"Unforgiveness is like drinking poison yourself and waiting for the other person to die."

There is so much truth in that and I would know firsthand. I never thought I was a person that held grudges until I was put in a position to forgive someone and extend for them to forgive me, by the orders of God. I fought hard, because I knew I wasn't wrong. I wanted the people that hurt and betrayed me to suffer. I wanted them to feel what I felt. I never said it out loud, because the reality is no one acts as if they have unforgiveness in their heart. But, I did for a while and at times some memories pop up and I find myself detouring back to those old feelings. Healing is a process. I had layers and layers of healing that I didn't even know I needed until God started showing me things in my healing season.

I needed healing from:

Unforgiveness I had with father figures
Unforgiveness I had with past betrayal
Unforgiveness from myself and what I allowed

There were many times when I knew it was time for me to heal but, because it just seemed too hurtful to bring up past situations and work on them I just buried it. I started to realize it was time to start healing when my mood would change around certain people. I'm talking about being so happy and then they would come into my space and my mood went from happy to instantly silent or angry. I started to realize I was robbing myself of my happiness by not working on my healing. It no longer had anything to do with them. I had to heal, I needed to heal from those things done to me. I needed God to move in my life, but I knew blessings couldn't be handed out my way until my healing began.

It can be difficult to have your healing time when you're trying to just live life like a normal twenty something year old. When you know where God is taking you or if you feel that it is time to start Bossin' Up your life, healing is a part of it all. I began my healing process by detoxing from social media and focusing on myself and being in solitude with God.

Healing 101: Things I Did to Heal

- Wrote down everyone's name who had hurt me or that I hadn't forgiven
- Grabbed sheets of paper and started writing Dear Letters to people that hurt me. This is where you will write Dear (add name) and say what you always wanted to say.

- I got ALL my anger out. Everything I felt. Things I never got the chance to say on that piece of paper.
- After, writing the letters to the people that hurt me, I found a quiet place, and then I acted as if the person was in front of me and I read it out loud. Some letters I read with anger, some letters I read with tears in my eyes. Whatever you feel in that moment while you're reading that letter out loud let yourself feel those emotions!
- Then here's the fun part. Rip up the letter after reading them. I ripped them up like I never ripped something up before. Some letters I ripped with so much anger, some letters I didn't.
- Whatever you feel in that moment while ripping up the letters, let yourself feel those emotions.
- Now breath! Slowly and deeply. Inhale and exhale twice and watch how you begin to feel!

I also wrote a letter to myself. I started off with "Dear Me..." and I told myself sorry for things that I allowed. I told myself that I was a good person, even when I didn't feel like it in certain situations. I gave myself an apology for staying in situations way longer than I should have. It is important that you also apologize to yourself. You may not even feel that the people that betrayed or hurt you deserve your forgiveness, and I totally understand because that was me in that situation. But, I was tired of always being angry and holding on to the same situation. I had to make a change, even if I felt that I was justified for feeling how I felt. You too need to make a change and begin forgiving. It is not for them; it is for you.

Forgiving 101

The truth is, I'm still learning how to fully forgive others because like I said, girl, it's hard. It is an everyday struggle, but it something that I work on and that you can work on as well.
Here are four ways that are helping me to fully forgive:

1. BE with the experience.

Shift your energy to being with the experience. Allowing yourself to feel what you're feeling (sadness, anger, hurt,) and understand it. A lot of times we as humans don't "be with the experience." We get upset or we're hurt, but we don't take the time to sit with it and understand why we really are. We don't examine how this truly makes us feel. Allow it all to unfold and then remind yourself that you have control over what you allow to control your emotions.

"I am in total control of what controls my emotions."

"Things can only change my mood if I allow it to."

"I am with the experience, I am feeling it, I understand it. I am becoming at peace with this situation."

2. **NO finger pointing mentality.**

I mean we can spend all day finger pointing every reason as to why this person was wrong (I mean sis, I literally used to have a list). You can spend all damn day showing evidence like you are in a *Law & Order* episode as to why this person is wrong, and why they should rot in hell for what they did to you, but it's not worth it. It is beyond draining. Because when you are done with throwing the evidence in their face to make yourself feel better, and justify your hurt and anger, and they still don't give you the "sorry" you want or change... then what? THEN WHAT? You're back to square one of feeling the anger, hurt, or sadness, you have been feeling.

3. **TAKE responsibility for your part.**

Here is where you have to get real with yourself. You might feel like why am I taking responsibility for my part? I'm the victim! I'm the one that is hurt dammit! But get honest with yourself. Has this person hurt you before and you allowed it? How many times did you allow it? How many times did you sweep their actions under the rug? Did you ever tell them how you felt the first time? And if they didn't change, did you cut them off or did you keep them around hoping they would change?

These are the REAL questions you need to ask yourself and I guarantee, you will realize like I had to, that you played a part in the situation.

4. **BE present.**

This is a big one I had to learn. Sometimes situations will keep popping in your head of past wrongdoings, and you continue to live in that moment of the past instead of your present moment. We cling onto those past hurts and replay it over and over but it happened, its done, you can't go back and change anything. Let it go and be present and at peace with where you are NOW! There ain't nothing like having your present robbed from you because you want to keep reliving past situations. THAT my friends is how you steal your own joy away from you!

Therapy 101

I even took my healing a step further and went to therapy. I am all about God being in my life, and praying to Him when things are rough, but I am also team therapy. Going to therapy and being able seek professional help when things are spiraling out of control is okay. There is nothing wrong with it. I know God put therapy in my path. My therapist was a woman who also believed in God and the guidance she gave me was as if God had put her on my path to deliver this help personally. Therapy was needed. There are layers to these healings. One day you will feel healed and ready to take on the world, and the next you'll be back to square one with the same feelings wondering how did you get back here? In order for me to snatch back my power this was the final test in my process of Bossin' Up. I found some of my peace in therapy. I found ways to handle the things that I was feeling. It was another form of layers being peeled off and showing me areas in my life where I can approve with the help of how to navigate with what I am feeling. Therapy was a way for me to talk to someone who knew nothing about the people that I was talking about. They didn't know me personally besides the hour that I was around them. I felt calm. I was able to talk and say what I felt and learn amazing lessons on how to look at my situations differently. Even things that I did not feel deserved my forgiveness at the time.

My therapist pointed something out to me when I told her I was struggling with forgiving some people that I felt betrayed me. She let me know of course that the forgiveness wasn't for them, but for me. I mean most of us know this, but do we understand it? I sure as hell didn't when I first walked in. Like, of course forgiveness is for me, but I simply couldn't just forgive these people. Through it all, she also reminded me when I think about certain situations that I have not shown forgiveness to, do the following:

1. Pray for them: Try praying for the person that hurt or betrayed you for 30 days straight
2. Remember the good times and say to yourself, "That was a good time in my life and I had that great memory with them, and I am thankful for that."

I struggled like hell with these two. Like, girl what do you mean pray for them and remember the good times, and be thankful for them? HELLO can't you tell that I am operating in anger right now? It was clear that what she was doing was helping my healing even further. I know you are probably thinking the same way that I was thinking; *there is no way in hell I am praying for someone that did me wrong.* I was beyond against it. Therapy at times was hard work, but it helped me dive deeper into what I needed to work on within myself. Once I started doing the homework that I was given in therapy, which included those two instructions, it was as if another weight was lifted off my shoulders. I had to genuinely pray for those people that caused me pain. And no not the prayer, "God, make them right cause you know they are the devil." More like, "God please bless them. Help them to see you in all things. God I ask that you cover them. I ask that you send blessings down on them. I also ask God that you help me to heal from past hurts from this individual. I ask whatever I may have done unknowingly that may have affected them that you heal them as well." Pray for their healing and happiness. It was hard. No one if we are being honest, wants to pray for people that wronged them. But, one thing that is for certain you can't keep drinking poison, such as holding on to anger or bitterness and praying that it destroys the people that did damage to you. The only person you are hurting is yourself.

I SNATCHED BACK MY: ***JOY***

It is important that you get this healing. It is important that you pray for others who come against you. It might not feel fair. You might want to see their karma because of how they did you, but where God is taking you, you cannot hold onto things such as this. You deserve a life of peace and happiness, but you can't do that if you don't take the time to work on you and your healing. It is time!

Who do you need to heal from?
(List their names below.)

_____
_____
_____
_____
_____
_____

What prayer would you say for that individual?

_____
_____
_____
_____
_____
_____
_____
_____
_____
_____
_____
_____
_____
_____

Healing 101:
Dear Self Letter

Dear Self,

Forgive yourself. Forgive yourself for everything. You are human. Everything you've been through or continued to stay in was teaching you something. Don't you dare change your beautiful personality, good energy, and forgiving heart. That makes you, YOU! I know that hurt got to you. I know you thought the people that turned on you would never do it. I know for a short period of time they had you questioning yourself and doubting if you were a good person. YOU ARE A GOOD PERSON! They do not have that power over you. Forgive yourself for speaking ill on others when they did you wrong. You were vibrating from a low frequency. Let go of that guilt of holding onto certain relationships longer than you should have even when God gave you sign after sign of who was for you and who was not. You see the good in people even when they do you wrong. Forgive them anyways. It is okay that you are like that, you just know moving forward when people show you who they are believe them the first time. Be gentle with yourself on this journey of healing. It is not easy *digging up old feelings and having to currently live them out, but you got this girl. You need this girl. God is ready to elevate you to the next level. You are learning. You are right where you need to be. Keep going, all the hurt and betrayal you felt is only to build you up. God knows what He is doing. He is trying to change something in your life. Hold on, everything will soon make sense. In the midst of all this, continue to shine your light. Continue to tell your truth. Someone needs it. You let yourself dim your light way too many times to makes others feel secure, don't EVER do that again. Regardless of what you go through girl, keep your power. Keep being confident in who you are. No one can break that, and even if they try this time you have God on your side. Forgive them, forgive yourself. You walk with your head held up high, you came too far to do otherwise. Continue to be you and you will attract the right ones in your life. The very people that tried to break you will soon realize that all they did was plant a seed that God was going to water. Keep going. Your story is going to come together beautifully. You won't fold, girls like you don't fold. Some life lessons may hurt right now and you may feel misunderstood and lost, but when you recognize the power you had all along you will learn how to start Bossin' Up. You been a boss; it's just time for you to tap into the power that you always had. This hurt you are feeling now will soon turn into healing. It is just going to take some time to heal. The healing process is not going to be easy. You will have to strip everything that became you off of you and get back to your authentic self. Friends will have to be let go during the process. You will have to forgive others. Stay silent and watch how God works in your life. Trust, when it all comes together you will sit back in amazement and all you will be able to do is say, thank you God. Thank you for the betrayal, thank you for the people "cutting me off," thank you for showing who was really for me and not for me, thank you for the healing, thank you for this process. You will start to understand the shift that had to take place. You will understand why God had to isolate you. You will understand why God had to take you through some painful experiences. Then, you will be ready to heal. SNATCH BACK YOUR POWER! You got this. The world needs your light. You need your light. And when I tell you, when you RISE UP you will rise up stronger than ever before. Believe me, you're about to shock everyone, including yourself. Remember, you happen to life. Life doesn't happen to you. I love you forever. I forgive you.*

* *

PRAYER

Dear God,

I need you more than ever. I am not in a place where I want to forgive these people. I am in a place where I want revenge. I want them to feel how I feel God. I am hurt. That betrayal hurt. That assassination of my character God, hurt. I AM HURT. God, I know who I am and who I am not, but for some reason I can no longer figure it out. Help me God, to forgive. Help me to have a heart more like you. Help me God, to be at peace with what was done to me, and still wish them well, and actually mean it.

Amen

AFFIRMATIONS:

I am attracting the right people into my circle.
I am a good person.
I forgive others and I am forgiven.
I am healing from past hurts day by day.
I am snatching back my JOY.

WALK IN YOUR TRUTH

"Speaking your truth is the most powerful tool we all have."
Oprah Winfrey

This is your time to walk in your truth. Speaking your truth is the most powerful tool that we have. You speaking your truth can help another person get through what they may feel only they are experiencing. This is why I wrote this book. I wanted you and other women to know that I too have been through some things, and although our journey may not be the same there are some similarities. I wanted to be able to share my wisdom and to be able to help you and other women begin tapping into their Bossin' Up season with God and see it in a different light. It is important that you walk in your truth and share that journey when you are ready. Someone out there is waiting for your obedience, for you to step into all of what God has for you.

Your obedience is tied to their breakthrough.

Walking in your truth is not always the easiest, because none of us want to share the moments where we had breakdowns. Where we questioned if this is even the path for us. Where we felt alone, but it is the process that God had you on to build you back up. He's putting you on this path to get to know Him better, so you can get to know you better. He's putting you on this path for the bigger picture. Someone needs your story to help them get through. There's no more sitting there letting life happen to you, no! YOU happen to life! You take back your joy, you take back your happiness, your laughter... SNATCH IT BACK!

The process is making you stronger.

You are in Divine Alignment in your process.

You are in Divine Creation in your process.

Once you begin to walk in your truth, God will begin to reveal things to you. The process He had to put you through will be for a reason. God is about to shift your life in a crazy way. You will look back and chuckle at the things you thought you couldn't overcome, but here you are. Overcoming shit. Your story is coming together beautifully. You are an amazing person. What you thought almost broke you, when others thought they broke you, you will soon look back and laugh because you thought too small of yourself and the power you had all along. The power of God involves turning things around for your greater good. Yes, it will take time to heal.

Hold your head up even through this time. Others see something in you that you do not see just yet, and that's why they have been trying to stop you. God is going to help you recognize what is on the inside. He is about to help you to learn how to fight. You will get your fight back. You didn't lose you, God is just building you up to the version that He is calling you to be. Your process (your truth) cannot be rushed. God is going to take you through, but the key is you are going to have to let God help you. This is your time, girl. Let this process happen so God can go ahead and begin Bossin' Up your life. Those prayers you are praying for elevation; God is ready but you can no longer fight His process. Walk in your truth even if you are shaking. He will build you up. He will help you snatch back YOUR power. He will begin Bossin' Up your life in many ways that you couldn't even imagine. See, you're special and He needs to show you how. And this is not only how you begin snatching back your power through this process of Bossin' Up, but He will also show you how to keep that power moving forward. You have to walk in your truth. Someone out there needs what you are too scared to share. Someone needs to hear this story so they too can know they're not alone. You know how that feels. God is giving you the wisdom and it is time you walk in your truth and share it with others.

Remember:

1. Hold your head up high during this process.

2. Carry all the wisdom God is giving you through your own process.

3. Remember to reach back and help someone up through their difficult time.

4. Never be ashamed of what God put you through in order for you to get to the Bossin' side.

You got this. This is your season to shine and begin Bossin' Up.

YOU ARE THE TRUE DEFINITION OF BOSSIN'

* *

PRAYER FOR YOU

Dear God,

Cover them as they are walking in their truth. Help them to remember all of the wisdom and good that came out of the process. Help them to walk into obedience in what you are asking them God. God, I ask that you let who is reading this be able to step into their full potential. Help them to recognize the authority they have over their life. God, help them to shine in a way that when they walk in the room people know that they are touched by you.

Amen

* * *

AFFIRMATIONS:

I am walking in my truth.
I am proud to share my truth.
God is giving wisdom everyday through this process.
I am changing lives with my story.
I am the definition of BOSSIN'.

About the Author

Ke'Arra Kelly is a 24-year-old, who has always been sassy, confident, and authentic in who she is. Ke'Arra graduated from one of the only two all-women's HBCUs, Bennett College in 2016 with a degree in journalism and media studies. While attending college Ke'Arra created two shows titled *Ke's Got the Tea* and *The Hashtag*, both focusing on celebrity and real life news. With having a great deal of experience in the media world, from working on red carpets and interviewing celebrities, to working in Production on ABC's hit show

Station 19, Ke'Arra saw firsthand how the media world worked. She realized something was missing.

After graduating Ke'Arra fell into a post graduate depression that made her question everything around her, even her career path. As things started to change in her life Ke'Arra found herself losing her passion for the media world that she worked in. Although she was grateful to have these experiences and working on a TV show that was known worldwide, she knew that there was more that she had to offer. As someone who had her life fully mapped out, Ke'Arra was immediately shaken up when she realized her life was not going as she planned.

Post graduate depression hit her like a ton of bricks and during the time, she felt like there was nowhere for her to turn. She didn't feel a sense of safe space like she did when she was at Bennett College. She needed that space to feel connected with others, heal, and just knowing that she wasn't in it by herself. After doing her own research and not finding anything that made her feel like this person gets me, she decided to create the space she so desperately needed. January 2017 Ke'Arra created Bossin' Her 20s. A blog focused on sharing her personal experiences and others, with no mask on. She gave the real on what she was going through. Ke'Arra needed a space that was authentic. An environment that was full of realness and authenticity. And she did just that with her own blog. It has not only helped her heal, but it was helping other women in their twenties who were experiencing the same issues heal and recognize their own power.

Ke'Arra is currently working on new projects and interning with Nia Sade Akinyemi assisting with helping other women of color tell their own stories through books for the world to see.

Ke'Arra's main goal is to keep creating spaces for women to know that everything isn't about that perfect filter moment we see play out time and time again on social media. Her main focus is to create a space where women feel free and safe to discuss what they too are experience. For them to heal and begin snatching back their own power.

Check out her blog here:
bossinher20s.com

Social media:

Instagram: @sweetkearra
YouTube: BossinKeArra

Made in the USA
Middletown, DE
23 July 2019